Smart Speaking

LAURIE SCHLOFF and
MARCIA YUDKIN

Smart
Speaking

. . . .

Sixty-Second
Strategies

Henry Holt and Company
New York

Published by Henry Holt and Company, Inc.,
115 West 18th Street, New York, New York 10011.
Published in Canada by Fitzhenry & Whiteside Limited,
195 Allstate Parkway, Markham, Ontario L3R 4T8.

Library of Congress Cataloging-in-Publication Data
Schloff, Laurie.
Smart speaking : sixty-second strategies / Laurie Schloff and
Marcia Yudkin. — 1st ed.
p.   cm.
Includes index.
ISBN 0-8050-1302-4 (acid-free paper)
1. Oral communication.   2. Public speaking.   I. Yudkin, Marcia.
II. Title.
PN4121.S284   1991
302.2′242—dc20   90-5292
                                                                      CIP

Henry Holt books are available at special discounts
for bulk purchases for sales promotions, premiums,
fund-raising, or educational use. Special editions
or book excerpts can also be created to specification.
For details contact:
Special Sales Director, Henry Holt and Company, Inc.,
115 West 18th Street, New York, New York 10011.

First Edition

Designed by Kate Nichols

Printed in the United States of America
Recognizing the importance of preserving the written word,
Henry Holt and Company, Inc., by policy, prints all of its
first editions on acid-free paper. ∞

10   9   8   7   6   5   4   3   2   1

To everyone everywhere
who ever took the time
to communicate
a little bit better

Contents

Preface   xiii

I Don't Like the Way I Sound

I'd Like to Have Crisp, Polished Speech Patterns
  —Like a Newscaster   3
I Sound So Boring!   5
I Say "Um" Too Much   7
People Often Ask Me to Repeat Myself   8
I Talk Too Fast   11
I Talk Too Slowly   13
People Can't Hear Me   15
People Complain That I'm Too Loud   17
Should I Lower My Pitch?   19
My Voice Sounds Too Nasal   21
People Tell Me I Sound Like Marilyn Monroe   22
When I Talk a Lot, My Voice Gets Tired   23
I Run Out of Breath When I Speak   25
When I First Open My Mouth in the Morning,
  Nothing Comes Out Right   27
I Hate the Way I Sound on Tape   28
Should I Try to Lose My Accent?   30
I Sound So Young on the Telephone, People Ask
  to Speak to My Mother   33
People Don't Think I Mean Business When I Speak   35

Conversational Blocks

I Never Remember People's Names After I'm
  Introduced   39
How Do I Break Into a Group of People Talking?   41
Can I Tell Beforehand If Someone Wants to Talk
  to Me?   43

Some People Can Begin Conversations Anywhere.
   Why Can't I? 45
I Hate Small Talk 47
How Do I Get Someone to Open Up? 49
I'm Never Sure Whether Someone Wants to Keep
   Talking to Me 51
I Don't Know How to Change the Subject When
   I'm Bored to Tears 52
I Can Never Think of Anything Clever to Say 53
My Conversations Always Seem to Die 56
I Don't Know How to End a Conversation 58
I'm a "Toucher," but I Know It Turns Some
   People Off 60
How Do I Approach a Famous Person Without
   Making a Fool of Myself? 62

Telephone Hangups

Is There a Best Way to Answer the Telephone at Work? 67
How Do I Get Past the Secretary? 69
What's the Nicest Way to Put Someone on Hold? 71
My Coworkers Bother Me When I'm on the Telephone 73
What If I Have to Get Someone's Attention in
   Thirty Seconds? 74
I Hate Calling People I Don't Know 76
I Always Forget What I Wanted to Say 78
Telephone Tag Is Driving Me Nuts 79
I Hate Leaving Messages on Answering Machines 80

Nerves

Is There a Quick Way to Get Rid of Nervousness? 85
I Can't Sleep or Eat for Days Before an Upcoming Talk 87
If Only I Could Relax . . . 90
I'm Afraid I'll Go Blank 94
What If I Do Go Blank? 95

What If They See I'm Nervous?   97

I Wasn't Nervous Beforehand, but When I Got Up
   There I Thought I Was Having a Heart Attack   99

I Get Freaked Out When an Audience Stares
   Blankly at Me   101

I Hate to Introduce Myself to a Group   103

My Presentation Is Next Week—Help!

I Do a Lot Better One-on-One   107

I Don't Know How to Organize a Talk   109

Should I Use Notes, Memorize My Talk, or What?   112

Where Should I Look When I'm Speaking to an
   Audience?   115

How Can I Make Good Eye Contact If I Need to
   Use a Script?   116

What Should I Do With My Hands?   118

Do I Need to Tell Jokes in a Presentation?   120

I Feel So Awkward After I'm Introduced   122

How Do I Warm Up the Audience?   124

Should I Use Visual Aids?   127

Microphones Intimidate Me   130

What's the Best Room Arrangement for a Presentation?   132

How Do I Get Audience Participation?   136

What If They Ask a Question I Can't Answer?   138

I Don't Know How to Handle Idiotic, Repetitive, or
   Hostile Questions   140

I Never Stick to What I've Prepared   143

I Was Doing My Best, and They Still Looked Half
   Asleep   145

I'm Not Funny, Eloquent, or Interesting—Is There
   Any Hope for Me?   148

Meeting Headaches

I'm Not Sure How to Lead a Meeting   153

What If I Have Only a Minute to Prepare Some
    Remarks? 155
I Hold My Opinions In and Then Someone Else Always
    Says What I Was Going to Say 157
We Waste a Lot of Time at Our Meetings 158
We Never Make Any Decisions at Our Meetings 160
What Do I Do When the Meeting Gets Off
    Track? 162
How Do I Excuse Myself to Go to the Restroom? 164
How Do I Handle Difficult People in Meetings? 165

Tough Situations

I Get Upset When I'm Criticized 171
Is There a Way to Give Criticism Without Hurting
    Someone's Feelings? 172
Should I Stretch the Truth at a Job Interview? 174
How Should I Sit During a Job Interview? 175
My Boss Is Always Bugging Me 177
I Can't Stand Having to Sell (a Product, Service, or
    Myself) 179
How Do I Tell Someone She's Not Up to Snuff? 181
My Colleague Always Stands Too Close 183
How Do I Tell Someone He's Doing Something
    Annoying or Inappropriate? 185
If I've Said Something Ten Zillion Times, How Can
    I Not Seem Bored? 187
How Can I Break a Date Without Damaging a
    Relationship? 189
How Can I Persuade Someone Who Argues With
    Everything? 191
I Never Know What to Say to a Friend Who
    Just Lost Someone 193
Why Do Some People Talk So Much, and How Can
    You Politely Shut Them Up? 195
How Do I Use an Interpreter? 197

I Want My Boss to Know My Accomplishments
    Without Blowing My Own Horn   199

Awkward Moments

I've Forgotten the Name of Someone Who
    Obviously Knows Me   203
I Dropped Spaghetti on My Shirt While at Lunch
    With Clients   205
How Do I Get My Foot Out of My Mouth?   207
She Told Me to Call, but Now She Doesn't Remember
    Who I Am   209
I Don't Like to Lie, and I'm Asked About Something
    I Heard in Confidence   211
How Do I Handle Prying Questions, Such as "How's
    Your Sex Life?"   213

We're Not Communicating

People Always Interrupt Me   217
I Ramble a Lot   219
I Always Get Blank Looks When I Speak   221
What Do I Do When We're Just Not Clicking?   223
People Say I Look Angry (Sad, Bored), but I'm Not   225
People Say I Seem Standoffish, but I'm Really Shy   226
I Get Embarrassed When I'm Complimented   228
I Try to Motivate My Employees, but They Seem
    to Be Intimidated   230
I Have Trouble Understanding Foreign Accents   232
Aside From Changing My Foreign Accent, Can I
    Help People Understand Me Better?   233
My Colleague Never Listens to Me   235
I'm Not a Good Listener   237

Index   239

Preface

Piano students are often introduced to Chopin's "Minute Waltz" with the explanation that the word *minute* in the title means small (mi-*NUTE*) and that they shouldn't try to play the piece in sixty seconds. Similarly, we hope you won't time your reading of our book with a stopwatch. By *Sixty-Second Strategies* we mean solutions that you can read quickly and apply immediately.

Whatever your profession, background, or level of experience, this book is for you if you'd like to be a confident, effective communicator. We have designed the book so that you can dive in anywhere and find quick assistance for your urgent communication problems. Occasionally you will see cross-references inviting you to turn to another section for further information.

Two premises have guided this work. First, good actions lead to good feelings, a philosophy put forward by the philosopher and psychologist William James about a century ago. Whenever you improve any aspect of your communication—such as the sound of your voice or the way you give criticism—you're likely to receive more satisfying responses from others.

The second premise comes from a thought expressed by the late psychologist Carl Rogers. When he was asked what makes people good at something—parenting, painting, doctoring, managing, anything—he replied that skills or techniques were never the most important factors. Skills, he said, are an implementation of attitudes. In other words, once you care about your client, your colleague, your conversational partner, communication skills are likely to follow.

There is a short but important list of people whose aid we'd like to acknowledge: first, Diana Finch, our agent, and Channa Taub, our editor at Henry Holt, for helping to bring the book into existence. Laurie would like to thank Robert Davine, Bonnie Lerner, Sybil Tonkonogy, Gertrude Schloff, Anne Tavel, and Mona Yaguda for useful insights, and her husband, Ed Horowitz, for being a special someone and computer adviser; special appreciation as well goes to Dr. Dennis Becker, president of The Speech Improvement Company, for being a superb communicator and an outstanding mentor. Marcia expresses gratitude to Joan Yudkin for legal advice, and Florence and Gila Yudkin for ideas and feedback.

If there are communication problems or questions you would like us to consider in a sequel, please contact Laurie at The Speech Improvement Company, 1614 Beacon Street, Brookline, MA 02146 (617-739-3330) or Marcia at WordRight, Suite 434, 20 Park Plaza, Boston MA 02116 (617-338-7953).

··········

I Don't Like
the Way I Sound

• I'd Like to Have Crisp, Polished Speech Patterns—Like a Newscaster

Media folks tend to have speech that is more polished than average—it's a requirement for a job on the air. Many media personalities have achieved speech mastery through coaching or courses in phonetics (the study of sounds) and extensive practice in precise articulation. Julia, an experienced radio news editor, wanted to move into news broadcasting but was told that her speech didn't sound professional. The news program director told her to "clean up" her speech before a public debut. As many people who speak for a living have learned, Julia needed to polish her speech with plosives.

Plosive Polish

Plosives are a group of eight sounds in English. As the name suggests, these sounds are made by a mini explosion of air in the mouth. The contact between the articulators (tongue, palate, lips, and so forth) builds up air pressure and then releases it. But enough technical stuff. All you really need to know are the eight sounds and how to use them.

The plosive sounds are:

b	ca*b*
p	ti*p*
d	lea*d*
t	ligh*t*
k	ba*ck*
g	bi*g*
ch	*ch*ur*ch*
j	*j*ud*ge*

To sound like a professional speaker, you want to explode (say with a release of air) these sounds just enough to create a brief stop in the flow of speech. Indeed, another name for the plosives is *stops*. Say each of the above words so that there is a small burst of air at the end. Feel the air by putting your hand in front of your mouth. Be careful not to exaggerate the effect, though.

Most of us have no trouble using plosives correctly when they occur at the beginning of words (*b*ase, *t*ry). The most important times to explode them, however, are when they occur at the end of a phrase of thought, as in:

> "Did you get tha*t*?"
> "I know I'm righ*t*."
> "It does wor*k*!"

and when you want a certain word to stand out:

> "Why no*t* try it?"
> "You can'*t* go wrong."

To increase your plosive awareness, listen to a radio or TV personality who speaks in the crisp way you admire. Catch as many plosive endings as possible and repeat right after your role model.

Say these plosive practice sentences four times, twice with crisp endings and twice without, until you feel and hear the difference.

> "This projec*t* will brin*g* new business to the marke*t*."
> "I li*k*e the way I soun*d* when I articula*t*e."

For everyday plosive practice, find an interesting magazine or newspaper column. Circle all plosives at the end of words. Record yourself and play back to see if you hit all your plosive targets.

> "Do i*t* righ*t*!"
> "I*t* won'*t* hur*t*."
> "Ge*t* i*t*?"
> "You can'*t* stan*d* i*t*."
> "This mus*t* sto*p*."
> "This is goin*g* to en*d* with better spee*ch*."

4

• I Sound So Boring!

Despite the twenty hours Luanne spent preparing for each lecture to her nursing class, her students consistently rated her as dull. Jacob, a mechanical engineer with innovative ideas and brilliant designs, could not keep any audience interested in his presentation. Luanne and Jacob suffered from the bane of being boring, perhaps the worst curse that can afflict a speaker.

Though you might think that people like Luanne and Jacob were born boring, the truth is that they just never learned certain speech habits that most of us pick up naturally. In working with hundreds of tiresome talkers, I have found that training in simple techniques of vocal variety usually does the trick.

Vocal variety is the skill of emphasizing certain words to convey meaning and emotion so that those words "jump out" at the listener. It is the vocal equivalent of a colorful gesture. The following tips will pull you—and the audience—out of the dull-drums.

1. *Pitch change.* Change your pitch (usually upward) on an important word or syllable. Practice these sentences with a higher pitch on the word indicated, noticing that you have the power to change meaning as you change pitch:

> "She's wearing a ↑*RED* dress" (not green).
> "↑*SHE'S* wearing a red dress." (*That* woman is.)
> "She's ↑*WEARING* a red dress" (as opposed to carrying or eating it).

Tape-record yourself and listen to make sure that the meaning really does stand out.

2. *Volume change.* Go louder on your most important word. You may feel as if you're shouting but trust me, it's just that

you're not used to adding that extra *oomph.* Or, for the "Mr. Rogers" approach, go softer.

Practice with this sentence:

"A *LONG* journey begins with a single step."

3. *Length change.* Admittedly a hammy technique. Ed McMahon has made millions introducing Mr. Carson with an extra long "Heeeere's . . ." Lengthen the vowel of a word to signal great interest or drama. For example:

"I dooon't see the point."
"He's aaabsolutely out of his mind."
"Brides don't neeeed to wear long dresses."

To practice vocal variety, pick a paragraph each day from the newspaper or a magazine. Underline the important words in every sentence. Be generous with yourself—don't try to become overly exciting suddenly. Tape-record yourself as you read the paragraph aloud and play it back to see if you actually "hit" the words you targeted.

Phil, an international marketing director who knew that he usually put his audience to sleep, contacted me before an important presentation. In our brief emergency coaching session we had time to work on only one skill, so we concentrated on vocal variety. He came into the session sounding nearly comatose and left sounding half alive. His boss must have agreed. He called me after Phil's talk to thank me, adding, and I quote, "Phil was 50 percent less boring than the year before!"

• I Say "Um" Too Much

Vocalized pauses or fillers, including *um, uh, ah,* and their close relatives *like, you know,* and *OK?* are some of the most common concerns brought to a speech consultant. We don't uh want to uh get too um picky here, since 1 to 3 percent of everyone's speech normally contains hesitations, and folks like Bobby and Ted Kennedy have spoken successfully in public life despite long *aah* pauses. However, a bad case of um-itis makes you annoying to listen to. So why do so many of us um along in life? Most often, vocalized pauses function as a way to fill up space as we formulate the next thought. Though old habits take some time to break, it *is* possible to banish the *um*s and *ah*s forever.

For Um and Uh Extermination

1. Spend a week observing your *um* and *uh* pattern. One client kept an *um* tally on her clipboard whenever she spoke at a meeting. Just becoming aware of the dimension of the problem helps you cut down.

Optional: Enlist the help of a friend to signal when you're using too many fillers in your everyday conversation.

2. Practice deliberately inserting silent one- or two-second pauses into your speech. Many people who *um* their listeners to distraction don't realize that short silences are less obtrusive and perfectly acceptable.

3. Your goal is to allow a slight pause instead of unnecessary vocalizing. Try to catch the start of *um* and *uh* (you can feel it in a movement of your vocal cords). Nip it in the bud and just be silent instead!

• People Often Ask Me to Repeat Myself

That must be frustrating for both you and your conversational partners because nobody likes talking or listening to be hard work. Let's first try to figure out where the snags are in your speech patterns.

Are you dropping your volume at the end of sentences?

It is normal to soften your volume at the end of a thought, but don't trail your sentences into oblivion. Assess your volume by taping yourself and checking to make sure you can hear the last words of your sentences. Practice speaking or reading aloud with conscious attention on lessening the decibel drop. Use these practice sentences:

> "Let's meet in the lobby of the downtown Marriott."
> "Sarah James was finally promoted to regional manager."

In these examples, if you don't keep your volume up, you'll be swallowing your main point. See "People Can't Hear Me" (page 15) for more suggestions on keeping your volume up.

If volume is not the problem, are you jumbling words together?

Some degree of assimilation, or blending sounds and words together, is normal in conversational speech. An example of assimilation is the phrase, "How are you?" The *ow* sound at the end of *how* naturally blends into the *a* in *are*, so the phrase sounds more like "Hower you?"

When sounds and words blend too much, clarity collapses in a condition specialists call overassimilation. Overassimilation makes it difficult for a listener to tell if you said "at you" or "ah choo," "we can" or "weekend."

Assimilation once even created problems for a large corporation. A chain of stores selling industrial clothing answered their telephones in the following way: *"Ritefit Work Clothes."* Company receptionists were puzzled because callers were constantly hanging up on them. The problem? Overassimilation. Callers were hearing *"Ritefit, we're closed."* Certainly a justifiable reason for hanging up!

You can find out if you tend to jumble your words by listening to a five-minute sample of a telephone call or conversation you have taped. If possible, ask a friend or relative to listen with you to provide objective feedback. Note any words or phrases that were difficult to understand. Pay particular attention to long words, names, and the ends of sentences.

If you are jumbling more than twice a minute, here is a starter list of words and phrases that are frequently assimilated. Practice saying them incorrectly, then correctly for contrast. Add additional phrases to the list as you observe yourself in everyday talking.

cancha	can't you
cudja	could you
generly	generally
havta	have to
howzitgon	how's it going
I dunno	I don't know
probly	probably
shuda	should have
uzhly	usually
wanna	want to
wuncha	wouldn't you

Another possibility: Are you moving your mouth enough when you speak?

Some speakers fail to put their best mouth forward due to reticence or a desire not to appear too outspoken. Robyn, an advertising agency president, wanted to accept offers to appear on panels at industry conferences, yet when in the spotlight, she gave the impression that her jaw was wired. During our first meeting she figured out why she became tight-lipped under stress. As a teenager she had tried to hide a mouthful of metal caps and wires whenever she had to speak to a class or appear in a play. Now that she had a straight set of teeth, Robyn needed to learn these two techniques of mouth mobilization:

Practice precision

Make precise movements on the following lip sounds:

b	*b*ank	la*b*
p	*p*ark	ta*p*
m	*m*oney	ti*m*e
v	*v*ote	dri*v*e
f	*f*irst	li*f*e
w	*w*in	wo*w*

Practice sentences (five times every day):

"Bob, please pass the proposal to Walt."
"Mona, would you make a copy of Fred's will?"
"Fred would live winters in West Palm Beach."

Vow to work on vowels

Most vowels require a degree of mouth opening (doctors ask you to say *ah* for a reason!), and they're great to practice opening that oral orifice. Say these vowels with as much stretch as possible. Start with the following words and sentences and then focus on the same vowels in everyday speech.

ah	stock	job
eh	met	bet
ae	cat	fat
o	no	open
aw	fall	talk
ow	mouth	out
ai	buy	deny

Practice sentences:

"How wide can you go?"
"Why open my mouth now?"
"I found the way."

• I Talk Too Fast

Some fast talkers come from families where there is a lot of competition for the floor. Fast talking was originally a way to get their parents' attention, and the habit stuck. Others come from families that seem to have a genetic speed streak—they walk fast, work fast, and also talk fast. Some people race-talk because they feel no one really wants to listen to them. They don't like to listen to themselves speak and want to get it over with as soon as possible. Finally, rapid speech can be a sign of stress. When your body is feeling great pressure, all your bodily rhythms speed up, including speech.

The good news about fast talking is that studies show listeners prefer a faster-than-average speaking rate to a slower-than-average rate. The bad news is that speaking at breakneck speed can leave a negative impression. If you are talking so fast that people find you hard to understand or wonder why you're so eager to "get it over with," start slowing down your speech with this technique:

1. Use the *One-Two* technique. Count "one-two" in your head at natural pauses between phrases, sentences, and items in a list. The extra second will help you control your breathing better and allow time for listeners to absorb what you've said. Example:

> "I'm glad to be meeting you today [one-two]. Before we get on with our agenda [one-two], I'd like to ask each of you [one-two] to introduce yourself [one-two] and tell us a bit about your company."

2. Practice the *One-Two* technique while reading a newspaper or magazine article aloud. Use a tape recorder to double-check that you've really allowed the pause it takes to say "one-two."

Once when I discussed speech improvement techniques at an attorneys' association, a young woman attorney came up to me afterward and said she wondered if it might be a good idea for her to talk fast. "Why?" I asked. "Because my clients are poor, and that way they get their money's worth," she said. "Well, not if the clients have to spend an extra half hour asking you to repeat what they didn't understand the first time," I replied.

Fast fact: According to the *Guinness Book of World Records*, John Moschitta of Boston is the world's fastest talker—545 words in just less than one minute in May 1988. Another Bostonian, John F. Kennedy, holds the record for speed speaking during an actual speech—327 words per minute in December 1961, while he was president.

• I Talk Too Slowly

If your conversational partner has mentally formulated her five-year business plan by the time you finish a sentence, or if your audience is tapping fingers and feet impatiently while you're finishing the first paragraph of your talk, it's safe to say you're too slow. A colleague told me he recently walked out of a lecture at a conference and demanded the return of his thirty-five-dollar registration fee. The reason? He clocked the speaker at ninety words per minute—about half the average speaking speed.

Some slow talkers do everything at tortoise pace, including speaking. Others take great pains with their speech because they believe everything that comes out of their mouth must be correct, perfectly worded, and significant. It's admirable to care about what you say, but if you speak too slowly, you may be perceived as boring, tired, or less intelligent than you are. To keep people awake and interested, learn to increase your speaking speed without losing articulation and thought clarity.

To Get Up to Speed

1. *Learn what makes you slow.* Record a one-minute monologue on tape. Use a stopwatch or second hand and listen for the following types of slow spots.

Problem One: too many words along the way to your point.

> "As I was mentioning yesterday when we met with um, ah, Anderson Industries about the takeover negotiations and ah, proceeded to come up with an alternate plan, I told you I'd be getting back to you, and so let me introduce our findings by saying . . ."

Better:

"Let me bring you up to date on our talks with Anderson Industries . . ."

Problem Two: a generally draggy pace, with both words and pauses drawn out. Audiences prefer an average rate of 180 words per minute or even a little faster.

Problem Three: pauses that are too frequent or too lengthy. Pauses between sentences or at the end of phrases should not last much longer than two seconds unless you're consciously pausing to let information sink in or for dramatic effect.

2. *Try these speed-up strategies.*

For Problem One: To practice getting to the point more quickly, ask yourself an opinion question. Using a stopwatch or second hand, give yourself forty-five, then thirty, then twenty seconds to supply an answer. This is a vital skill for any media appearance.

For Problem Two: To pick up the pace, choose a passage from a magazine or book of about 180 words. Practice reading it aloud, seeing how close you can get to finishing it in one minute without sacrificing meaning or clarity.

· For Problem Three: Accept that in most situations it is not necessary to deliver a perfectly shaped gem worthy of *Bartlett's Familiar Quotations.* Imagine your words pedaling the wheels of a bicycle: If you drop the pace too drastically, you'll fall over. Practice keeping up momentum with a story or explanation you know well. Then practice keeping up momentum while answering questions that you're posing to yourself for the first time.

If you are absolutely convinced that choosing perfect words is critical, then during longer pauses give nonverbal signals that you're thinking deeply: Remove your glasses, furrow your brow, drop your gaze, or turn slightly away from the audience. Take a cue from one of my professors who had a compelling presence despite slow speech and frequent pauses. Usually he paced as he taught, gesturing with chalk or a cigar and giving the impression that he was thinking with his entire body.

• People Can't Hear Me

The ability to speak softly can be an asset in many situations—when you want to comfort someone, for example, or when you want to project an image of gentle strength. Fred Rogers of *Mister Rogers' Neighborhood* proved that you can keep even small children's attention by coming on like a breeze rather than a barrel of monkeys. Whatever your desired image, however, people can't listen to what you say unless they can hear what you are saying. If people often ask you to speak up or don't respond when you speak, you probably need to learn to achieve greater volume.

Sometimes people unconsciously use a soft voice so they won't be heard. Joseph, a management consultant, had to give brief periodic progress reports to his boss, a partner in the firm. At one meeting his boss remarked that Joseph seemed "mousy" when he talked about his work. After we discussed the issue, Joseph concluded that he had a habit of lowering his volume when speaking to authority figures. In his convoluted attempt to "hide any mistakes he might have made" (although in truth his work was exemplary), Joe made the biggest one: He gave the impression of being too meek or, as he put it, "not real management material."

How to Speak and Be Heard

1. *Volume variation.* When you are alone, experiment with your volume potential to see what you're capable of. Without straining your vocal muscles, say the phrase "I feel fine" as if you're speaking to someone three feet away, at the other end of a long conference table, a room away from you, and then half a block away.

See "I Sound So Young on the Telephone, People Ask to Speak to My Mother" (page 33) for advice on how to project.

2. *Enlist a friend or colleague to be your coach* for a five-minute conversation across a medium-sized table. Tell her to signal a need for greater volume by raising an index finger. Do the same exercise with your eyes closed to help you develop a feel for your ideal volume. This time your coach can signal with a verbal cue such as "volume" or "more." Ask your coach to note any pattern of inaudible volume: You might have a habit of lowering your volume at the beginning or end of sentences or when you're speaking about yourself.

3. *Advanced level.* Repeat the previous exercise with a radio or TV playing in the background. This will help you adjust volume for a noisier environment.

4. *You want the support for volume* to come from a relaxed, open throat; breathing focused in the abdominal area; and a mouth kept as open as possible as you speak. Observe and evaluate those checkpoints as you project the following phrases with adequate volume to a spot in the room ten feet away:

> "My throat is relaxed."
> "I'm breathing deeply and relaxed."
> "My voice is filling my mouth."

Note: Aim for a pleasant volume without yelling or straining. Think of how Ronald Reagan is able to be heard without being the slightest bit harsh.

• People Complain That I'm Too Loud

Most of us instinctively do a good job of setting our volume so that it takes into account the distance between ourselves and listeners, the amount of background noise, and the degree to which we want to broadcast our message. Others, like one client who was known as "The Megaphone" in his office, don't do so well at this. Ernie came to see me when he realized that colleagues were requesting the cubicle farthest from his. One pal complained that he could hear Ernie's conversations better than his own. Ernie got the message "loud and clear" that his excessive volume was an office nuisance. He was receptive to working on his problem, though he was a little bit puzzled. He considered himself the quietest one in his family of five brothers.

To Adjust Your Volume Control

1. *Test it out.* Since poor ability to monitor and control volume could be an effect of hearing loss, rule out this possibility first via an audiological screening. Consult your family doctor, an ear, nose, and throat specialist, or an audiologist to schedule a hearing test.

2. *Tune in.* If your hearing is normal, ask a colleague or friend to help you discover your best conversational volume by signaling when your decibel level becomes deafening. Bring a tape recorder to a meeting and note how your volume compares to that of others.

3. *Try it on.* Contrast different volumes by saying words and phrases at various settings: softer than average, average, loud, and very loud.

> Single words: "Why, now, go, bye."
> Phrases: "Is this loud? I can control my volume."

Remember that your "soft" may be everyone else's "normal," and so on. Your goal is to begin to develop a sensitivity to the range of volumes and an internal sense that lets you know when it's time to tone down.

4. *Take it around.* Use your new, softer volume in routine situations, such as answering the telephone, greeting people, making a request. Notice people's reactions. If your listeners used to cringe and now you get no reaction, that's an excellent sign.

For advanced volume control, choose one five-minute situation a day in which to monitor your volume. You'll then be ready to use volume monitoring in the most stressful situations: when you're angry, emotional, or caught off guard.

• Should I Lower My Pitch?

People consider a lower pitch more authoritative and influential, though this perception is probably sexist in origin. Men naturally have lower pitch, and since they have held most leadership positions throughout history, we unconsciously associate a deep voice with power or strength. More and more female professionals, fearing that their usual voice pitch undermines their power and potential, have decided to try for a lower pitch.

Irma, a stressed-for-success defense attorney, came to see me after several embarrassing incidents in court. At particularly important moments her vocal cords would tighten, and she would experience a sudden and sharp rise in pitch. The last time this occurred she was in the middle of the sentence, "My client is not guilty," and the word *not* came out almost in a screech. Even the placid judge looked a bit startled at her ear-shattering jump in pitch. Irma needed to learn to control her vocal cord tension, particularly under stress.

This problem does not affect women only. Men with high-pitched voices are also often penalized. When talking movies replaced silent films, the careers of several screen idols took a steep slide to Nowheresville. They had manly looks but voices that were rather high. Directors and moviegoers weren't willing to tolerate the inconsistency.

Other people try so hard to make their voice deep that they develop a tired, crackly sound known as a "fry." Imagine a froglike "rib-it" sound or one so close to the lower limit of what the voice can produce that it sounds like a radio not quite tuned to a station. Not only does this sound unpleasant, it can damage the vocal cords. Henry Kissinger often pushes his voice into a "fry."

It is important for each of us to find the pitch that best suits our particular physical structure and desired image. But since changing your pitch will affect the functioning of your vocal cords, don't try for any dramatic changes in pitch without first consulting a speech-language pathologist with specific training in voice therapy. She will probably ask you to see an oto-laryngologist (ear, nose, and throat specialist) as well. But the following tips can get you started.

How to Tell If Your Pitch Is Too High

1. People mistake you for the wrong age and sex. One businessman told me he was sick of being called *Mrs.* rather than *Mr.* Zachary.

2. No matter what you say, you aren't taken seriously.

3. To find out what may be your best or most comfortable pitch, say the phrase "uh-huh" without effort. If it sounds much lower than the pitch you normally use, it's possible you're speaking at a higher level than you need to. You can also use this technique in a stressful situation. Find your optimum pitch by saying "uh-huh" out loud or mentally, and then begin your speech on that note.

Remember: Seek professional guidance before making any major changes in your pitch level.

To Make the Best of the Pitch You Have

1. Avoid dramatic upward shifts in pitch, like Irma's. They tend to give the impression that you are overly emotional.

2. In professional speaking, use the lower end of your pitch range. Stay at a point that allows pitch flexibility but not so low that you hear that tired "fry" sound.

3. Know the times when you are vulnerable to a pitch shift due to stress or nervousness. Be particularly aware of beginning on your "uh-huh" optimum note at these times.

• My Voice Sounds Too Nasal

Many sports fans believe that the all-time most irritating voice belongs to announcer Howard Cosell. One of the reasons his voice grates on people's nerves is that it is very nasal. In fact, most people rate nasal voices, where too much air escapes from the nose while speaking, as unpleasant or irritating.

In some cases, nasality results from a physical problem, such as a hearing impairment (that prevents effective monitoring of voice quality) or a cleft palate. It can also be due to tension or to influence of a local dialect (the nasal twang of Texas, the strong New York vowels as in p*aaa*nts). Most speakers can reduce their nasality by directing their voices differently. If you are nasal, you need to give your voice an exit route through your mouth, not your nose. These tips will help you reroute your voice energy and sound more pleasant.

To Reduce Nasality

1. Say the syllables *hi, hay,* and *how* gently. Put a hand in front of your mouth to feel the breath coming out orally.

2. Purposely tense up and say the same syllables nasally. You will feel more air coming out of your nose and less through your mouth. Notice the contrast with the gentle oral pronunciation. Repeat the sequence of 1 and 2 five times.

3. When you can deliberately control the difference between nasal and oral sounds, you are ready to use your most pleasant voice in real-life situations. For starters, use a relaxed oral sound when you say these words in everyday life: hello, how, who, why, bye, please, thanks, so.

4. Use this practice phrase to find your comfortable oral tone each morning: I like the sound of a pleasant open voice.

Note: The sounds *m, n,* and *ng* are supposed to be nasal, so don't try to make them through your mouth!

• People Tell Me I Sound Like Marilyn Monroe

If you sound like Marilyn, you'll make out much better in the bedroom than in the boardroom. Marilyn's voice, like Jacqueline Kennedy Onassis's, had a quality known as breathiness. This quality makes women sound feminine, secretive, coy, or sexy.

The increased intimacy that breathiness implies works less against men than against women. Ronald Reagan, known as "The Great Communicator," has the ability to use a breathy quality ("Well . . .") to sound personal and chummy when talking to 230 million people. Reagan's voice couples breathiness with a rich (not thin) tone, an appealing combination.

If your voice tends to be loud or nasal, breathiness can soften its unpleasant edge as long as you don't overdo it. Also, if you are dealing with someone who is soft-spoken or shy and you're not, breathiness can make your whole image gentler.

The cause of breathiness is the escape of air before the voice is activated. If you let out a little air and then say the word *hi*, you'll generate a breathy sound. To eliminate a breathy quality from your speech, try to:

1. Coordinate beginning to exhale with beginning to speak. Practice with the words *hi, my, go, no*.

2. Maintain audible volume throughout each word. It's hard to be breathy and loud at the same time.

• When I Talk a Lot, My Voice Gets Tired

The human vocal mechanism does not come with a lifetime guarantee against wear and tear, and some of us are more vulnerable to breakdown. If you talk a lot, like many teachers or salespeople, or speak with a lot of force, like cheerleaders or construction foremen competing with machinery in the background, you have to be especially protective of your vocal health.

Gail, a teacher and basketball coach, loved the action and pace of her job. Too often, however, her voice gave out before the game was over. After her physician prescribed a period of voice rest, she took action to reduce the stress she was placing on her voice. One of the most important things she did was purchase a portable microphone to use during coaching sessions. She reported that it was a pleasure to be able to keep the team's attention from the sidelines without shrieking.

Warning Signs of Voice Trouble

1. Your voice sounds or feels sore or tired.
2. You sound hoarse.
3. You feel you have to strain to get your voice out.
4. You lose your voice intermittently.

Important: If you experience any of these symptoms longer than ten days, be sure to consult a physician.

To Maintain Maximum Vocal Health

1. Love your larynx—stop smoking. Each year on the American Cancer Society's National Smokeout Day I throw a "Love Your Larynx" party to celebrate the day I gave up smoking years ago.

2. Stay out of smoky or otherwise irritating environments.

3. Don't scream. At a football game, just pretend you're screaming. No one will notice.

4. Avoid clearing your throat and coughing, as well as making funny Donald Duck or other cartoon sounds.

5. Watch out for trying to talk above the din in noisy environments. One client wanted to have meaningful conversations in bars but found that she ended up with chronic hoarseness. The only solution was to save the meaningful mingling for quieter rooms.

6. Keep your throat moist by sipping liquids before, during, and after extensive use of your voice. Avoid ice-cold drinks, though, which can tighten your vocal muscles.

7. If you talk a lot, control your rate and volume. Avoid straining your voice, that is, bringing your vocal cords together with too much force. Speaking in a more gentle and flowing manner is less likely to cause a vocal breakdown.

8. Give your voice a chance to rest each day.

• I Run Out of Breath When I Speak

If you are physically healthy, without any respiratory or other problems that might affect your air supply, you have more than the amount of air you need to speak—unless you happen to be jogging, climbing six flights of stairs, or engaged in passionate lovemaking while you're trying to say something. If you are sitting in the office and still run out of breath, you're probably making one of the following mistakes in the way you use your air supply:

1. You don't have enough breath support because your breathing is centered in your upper chest rather than your abdomen. Under stress many of us take much shallower breaths than we should.

2. You're taking too many breaths, overly concerned that you'll run out of air. By overcompensating you lose control over the air you are taking in.

3. You're exhaling most or all of your air and then proceeding to speak. That won't work because our speech needs to ride on the air as it is exhaled.

Norma, an air traffic controller who found the responsibilities of her job stressful, always sounded hurried and robotlike because she used little breath support for her speech. At the end of her sentences a trained ear could hear a quick gush of air expelled. She would inhale again, mistakenly hold that breath, speak, and then expel another gush of air. Norma needed to relearn the basics of breathing and speaking, skills we pick up naturally as children. After practicing the strategies below, she commented, "What a relief to know I can speak and breathe at the same time!"

Tips for Easy Speaking and Breathing

1. Get back to basics. Observe relaxed, deep, abdominal breathing patterns in yourself and others. Watch the rise and

fall of a baby's abdomen as she sleeps or your own abdominal breathing when you are stretched out in a warm tub or relaxed in bed.

2. Transfer that relaxed breathing pattern—inhale, abdomen out; exhale, abdomen in—to situations outside the tub or bed. You do not have to try it in stressful speaking situations yet. One thing you can count on is having plenty of opportunities to breathe (about twelve to eighteen cycles per minute for the rest of your life).

3. Start to build your breathing and speaking coordination. Try beginning to speak when you begin to exhale. Your goal is to spread your breath efficiently over the phrases. You should not run out of air before the end of the phrase, nor should you have a lot of air left over. Use the following increasingly longer sentences for practice.

> "Hello."
> "Hello, I'm here."
> "Hello, I'm here and breathing."
> "Hello, I'm here and breathing correctly."

4. Practice effective breathing daily. Choose an article from a newspaper or magazine and mark in advance the spots for a natural pause for breathing. Remember to initiate speaking at the beginning of an exhalation and to let your voice ride on the exhalation. Here is a marked paragraph to get you started. The slashes indicate where you should begin a new inhalation. Practice this way and then introduce your own variations to suit your style of speaking.

> Congratulations./You've achieved control over your breathing./You don't waste air/and you don't hold air in./At first it will feel strange./Then, with practice,/coordination will be more natural./Good luck!/You're on the right track!

• When I First Open My Mouth in the Morning, Nothing Comes Out Right

Morning mouth afflicts many of us who don't come alive until after lunch. Our mind-over-mouth ability suffers when our body would rather still be dreaming than debating. Since speaking involves precise muscular coordination, concentration, and alertness, why not think of yourself as a speech athlete each morning? Wake up and warm up your speaking mechanism with these exercises.

1. *The opening exercise.* Open your mouth as wide as possible and slowly close it ten times. Can you feel a stretch at the corners of your mouth? Lick your lips first if they feel dry. Note: Unlike no-pain-no-gain exercises, this should be painless. If it hurts, don't do it.

2. *The "kiss and smile" exercise.* Say *oo* as in *toot,* then *ee* as in *deed* in quick succession ten times. Good! Now you have stretched your lips to the limit.

3. *Mind-over-mouth quickie.* While dressing or combing your hair, think of a question you might be asked that day. Take fifteen seconds to come up with three key points you'll make. Take another thirty seconds to say your answer out loud.

You're ready to get out there and speak to win. Total mouth motorizer time: about a minute and a half. Make a copy of the exercises to tape on your bathroom mirror.

• I Hate the Way I Sound on Tape

In my work with hundreds of clients, including professional speakers such as actors and radio announcers, I have met only a handful who like the sound of their voice on a tape recorder. Some people even refuse to leave a message on an answering machine, knowing there would be a permanent record of their "awful voice" floating around in the world. Many speakers are certain that the taping distorts their voice.

I don't want to ruin your day, but the voice you hear on tape is the closest thing to the "real" you that you'll ever hear. That is because the tape recorder hears you as others do, through sound waves projecting into the air. When you listen to your own voice while speaking, you hear vibrations within your skull along with the vibrations in the air. That's why the voice you hear on tape is never like the one you're used to. A good goal for developing a pleasant and influential sound is to stop cringing every time you hear yourself on tape and make peace with your unique voice.

So the next time you hear yourself on tape:

1. Step back and ask: Do I sound *bad* or just *different* from the way I thought I would?
2. Notice at least one *good* point about the way you sound (it is loud enough; the pronunciation is clear; I sound easygoing).
3. Pick a specific way you would like to improve (I would like my voice to be softer, less whiny, deeper).

Tip: Try to *describe* (I was a little too soft) rather than *judge* what you hear (I sound like Minnie Mouse!).

If you are truly adventurous, you can improve your speaking voice—and perhaps even come to like how you sound—by bugging yourself ten minutes a day. Record yourself speaking on the telephone or bring a small tape recorder with you to important speaking events. Microcassette recorders fit right into a pocket, handbag, or briefcase.

Play back the ten-minute tapes, listening to and evaluating how you sound and noting changes that occur with different people and situations. When I play back tapes for my clients, I hear my own voice as well, so I now know exactly what to do to sound good on tape—and in real life.

After fifteen to thirty recording sessions, you'll develop a neutral attitude toward the sound of your voice and be able to be more analytical about its positive and negative aspects. And from then on you'll see the tape recorder simply as a tool, not as torture.

• Should I Try to Lose My Accent?

Because an accent reflects the sounds and patterns of a particular part of the country, the term "regionalism" is often used to describe speech linked with the area: New York, the South, Chicago, or wherever. It is indeed possible to lose the telltale traces of your native area, though children are usually much quicker at dropping or picking up accents than adults. You will need to ask yourself first whether you would really benefit from the change.

Consider regionalism removal if:

1. *Your speech pattern causes embarrassment.* Jack, a reserved Boston executive, participated in a Midwest conference with fifteen other company vice presidents from all over the country. Near the end of the work session he politely announced that he was leaving to go to the "party." His colleagues exploded with laughter. Their translation of Jack's Boston accent, where speakers weaken *r*'s after vowels, was that he was excusing himself to visit the "potty." Not very executivelike of him!

2. *Your speech pattern interferes with social or career success.* Though no accent is inherently better or worse than another, certain stereotypes are unfortunately attached to certain accents. People from other backgrounds often perceive a strong Southern drawl, a harsh New York area sound, or Black English as sounding uneducated. Job discrimination, conscious or unconscious, may result. One study showed, for example, that blacks who used standard English patterns rather than Black English patterns during job interviews were more likely to be hired.

Perry and Nadine, a couple who moved from Birmingham, Alabama, to Connecticut, came to see me because of their concern that they weren't being taken seriously in their computer industry managerial jobs. Perry said that the only advantage of his Southern accent was that people always seemed to be surprised when he offered a quick solution at a meeting. Apparently they assumed that he thought as slowly as he spoke.

But remember that regionalism can be an asset, not a liability, in some fields. Consider how the accents of Barbra Streisand, the Beatles, Dr. Ruth, and Jimmy Carter add to their appeal.

In the best of worlds, different accents merely reflect our diversity. Certainly if we all spoke with the same patterns, our country's melting pot would lose some of its spice. But if your regionalism is holding you back in the real world, consider a change.

3. *Your speech pattern annoys you.* It seems that every time I visit my family in New Jersey, the accent in the air grows stronger and stronger. I'm glad I have worked on softening my vowels in such words as *pants, bad, call, time,* and even the *a* in my hometown of Cranford. Losing much of my regionalism makes it easier for clients from all over to feel comfortable with me, without my New Jerseyese being the first thing noticed.

If you're considering working on your accent, first make an objective assessment of how you sound. Listen to yourself on tape. Ask for feedback from friends and colleagues, and decide if your accent is working for or against you. Because it takes expertise to analyze the unique rhythms, sounds, and emphases that make up your accent, you will need professional help if you decide to change. Look for a speech-language specialist who has studied phonetics. An effective accent modification program includes the following steps:

1. *Initial assessment period.* The specialist analyzes your speech patterns, compares them to standard American speech, and gives you specific examples of differences. Examples: "When there is a *th* sound at the beginning of a word, you say it more like *d*." "In American English there are more changes in pitch than you use."

2. *Discrimination instruction.* The specialist teaches you to hear the differences between the way you speak and standard

patterns and then to produce the standard patterns. If some sounds are new to you, the specialist will show you how to use your mouth, tongue, and breath to produce the sounds correctly.

3. *Practice and feedback.* Tapes help you practice at home. You should be able to make slight modifications in your accent after several sessions with a specialist, while a complete accent overhaul may require four to six months.

• I Sound So Young on the Telephone, People Ask to Speak to My Mother

Many factors affect the "age" of our voice. Structural abnormalities or, for men, a failure to complete a voice change in puberty may be discovered by a physician as causes. Then there is the psychological component. Some of us retain a young voice as a way of hanging on to a childlike side or self-image. Others simply never picked up on how to use their vocal equipment in an adult way.

Glen wanted to open his own antique dealership but wondered, after viewing himself on a friend's videotape, if his weak, wimpy voice would be a hindrance to his plan. We began a voice enhancement program, and with much trial and error, Glen began to sound his age. In addition to speaking at a lower pitch and maintaining adequate volume, Glen learned to enrich his voice. "Most people use only 50 percent of their voice power," he commented to me after much improvement. If you want to sound your age, you will need to work on adding richness to your voice.

How to Sound at Least As Old As You Are

1. *Rich resonance.* Resonance is the enhancement of your voice by using the space above your vocal cords as an acoustic chamber. Instead of sending out your sound through a narrow channel, picture your mouth as a cave that you fill up with your voice. Notice changes in your voice quality as you use 25 percent, then 50 percent, then 75 percent, and finally 100 percent of the space in the cave. Practice with the following syllables:

eye   why   bye   now   find

Never strain your vocal cord muscles to get more power.

2. *Power projecting.* Good projection means getting your voice where you want it to go with minimum effort and maximum quality. Visualize a fat arrow reaching from your mouth to an object three, then six, then ten feet away. Your goal is to have your voice effortlessly fill the arrow. For more motivation, picture a target (like a pot of gold) awaiting your voice at the end of the arrow.

3. *Standing up for yourself.* You will probably find it easier to use more of your voice if you stand rather than sit while you talk on the telephone. Standing may allow for better breath support, resulting in a stronger, richer voice.

4. *Little big man exercise.* Without any strain, say the following words and phrases, alternating between sounding as young as you can, using your usual voice, and sounding more mature and influential:

> "Hi."
> "How are you?"
> "What's new?"
> "I sound fine."

Observe the changes that take place in your voice as you do so. Of course, tape-record yourself when you try on different voices for size. There is likely to be one that fits just right.

• People Don't Think I Mean Business When I Speak

People will think you mean business if you communicate business. You can reinforce your authority by eliminating these undermining habits of speech:

Hedging and apologizing
You take your message back before you finish saying it.

> *Toss out:* "I don't know if you like getting comments, but I thought it would be helpful just to let you know, if it's OK, how the ad came across."
>
> *Substitute:* "I think the ad colors could be livelier."

Qualifying
You lessen the importance of your thoughts by adding "kind of," "sort of," and "just," ad nauseum.

> *Toss out:* "I sort of, well, I kind of wish you'd just maybe think about the customers a little bit more."
>
> *Substitute:* "You're paying a lot of attention to the other staff and not enough to the customers."

Raising your pitch at the end of a statement
Women do this more than men, and it sounds tentative and insecure.

> *Toss out:* "I'm sure you know what I mean? If not, I'd be happy to demonstrate?"
>
> *Substitute:* "I'm sure you know what I mean. If not, I'd be happy to demonstrate." (Pitch should drop at the end of a sentence to signify the end of a statement.)

Giggling and smiling too much
This is a special problem after a serious comment. Fiona, a young assistant professor with a Phi Beta Kappa brain, was notorious among her students for a peculiar habit. Every time she made a particularly astute observation, she would conclude the sentence with a giggle. In our work together she realized she giggled for fear that her high intellect would alienate students. She needed to learn that it was possible to be smart *and* well liked.

Purposeless moving and squirming, poor eye contact, head tilting, and fiddling with things
While gestures and animation can enhance the aura of leadership, adolescent hyperactivity diminishes it.

Scrunched-up posture
People who look influential spread out in space and relax. Dr. Donnelly, an ambitious radiologist, worked with me on his communication style in order to develop a memorable presence when he gave seminars. Though he was six-foot-one, he stood with his head stooped and his shoulders slouched, creating a less than regal presence. As we discussed his tendency to shrink in professional communication situations, he recalled that as a young teenager he had been much taller than his friends and so was nicknamed Stringbean. No one was about to mock his height now, and Dr. Donnelly learned to assume the physical posture to match his professional stature.

Thin vocal quality and high pitch
These two vocal traits produce a "not ready for prime time" image in the business world. Pee-wee Herman pee-wees well but does not come off as a mover and shaker. George Bush, you will recall, nearly sabotaged his 1988 presidential campaign with a high, strained, and uncontrolled vocal pitch. Until he received vocal and media training, he suffered from the label "wimp."

....

Conversational
Blocks

• I Never Remember People's Names After I'm Introduced

People with a good memory for names are not mental wizards, but they do devote more mental energy to remembering them than those of us who suffer temporary amnesia at the sight of Bill-Phil-or-was-it-Will. The cure for name amnesia is a foolproof, easy-to-apply memory strategy—that you won't forget to use. Here is one you'll remember by *N-A-M-E*.

In the *N-A-M-E* technique, each letter of the word *Name* stands for an important step in remembering who you just met.

Name grabber. After you meet, say the person's name aloud ("Nice to meet you, Sam") and then to yourself. If you aren't sure, now is the time to ask for clarification ("Do you go by Sam or Samuel?").

Attend and associate. The most critical phase! Devote five to ten seconds to focusing internally on the name and associating it with an image that the name reminds you of. For Sam, your association could be:

> Same name as Mona's husband (picture him).
> Picture your uncle Sam from Portland.
> Picture America's Uncle Sam.

Allow the association to be silly, outrageous, insulting, or whatever comes to mind. What matters is that it is meaningful and memorable to you. After the meeting, write down the name and your association.

Memory storage. Concentrate on your image for five seconds, seeing Uncle Sam or whatever you chose paired with the new person's face. In this way when you see What's-his-name again at the next Christmas party, Uncle Sam—and this person's name—will pop into your mind.

Two stockbrokers who were often stumped when it came to remembering clients' names used this technique to recall the names of thirty-five strangers' faces in a yearbook within one hour of learning the technique. Their enormous memory storage capacity shocked them because the day before they had had a hard time remembering the names of *three* clients right in front of them.

Exercise. Don't be lazy. To practice, try using the *N-A-M-E* technique in at least one business or social situation a day. For fun, try to memorize the names of characters on TV shows (for example, the first and last names of every character on *L. A. Law*) or names in the news (all the current cabinet members).

• How Do I Break Into a Group of People Talking?

Go easy on your expectations here. A group of people who have been chatting awhile have already put energy into establishing a conversational rhythm. So when a newcomer appears, the group minimizes having to adjust or backtrack by politely but slowly easing in a new conversational contender. If you have concluded that breaking into a conversational group can be difficult, you're right. But the cause usually is not rudeness, just a desire to continue a momentum that is satisfying.

I prefer the term "joining a group" rather than "breaking in" because your attitude needs to be adaptive, not aggressive. The degree to which the group resists an outsider depends on the intimacy shared by the conversers, their previous bonding as a group, and the group's perception of your status relative to theirs. For example, a college student walking over to a group of professors who are conversing will most likely get a brief, polite response, then a buzz-off signal as the profs continue to talk shop.

Loretta was eager to befriend a group of women she noticed having lively conversations in the cafeteria at work. One day she sat a seat away from them at a long table, hoping to be included in their conversation. When they didn't speak to her, she said she felt humiliated and dropped the idea of pursuing contact with them. Too bad! If she had hung in a bit longer, Loretta might eventually have made some new friends. She needed a better grasp of . . .

How to Get In With a Group

1. Don't expect to be greeted like Princess Di. Expect little more than a slight acknowledgment that you have arrived.

2. Be as unobtrusive as possible. Stand slightly away from the group but show interest in the speaker. Let them get used to the sight of you. Eventually everyone will shift to accommodate you.

3. Don't volunteer opinions or profundities right away. Your first remarks should acknowledge or agree with the speaker. If you sweep right in full force, they'll feel you are intruding—as you are.

4. Watch for signs that the group is opening for you. In addition to shifting positions to let you in physically, they may request your opinion or direct questions to you.

5. Ease into the conversation by showing you've been listening awhile: "Joe, I know what you mean about the movie being sentimental. It's almost as sappy as that French film I saw last week . . ."

Note: Sometimes it's wiser not to try to break into a group. Loretta would undoubtedly have been more successful approaching one of the women in that group who chanced to sit down early and alone. When the others joined the two of them, Loretta would probably have been included naturally, and the ice would have been broken for later occasions.

• Can I Tell Beforehand If Someone Wants to Talk to Me?

Initiating conversation would seem less risky if a crystal ball could tell us with whom we'd hit it off. Jackson, a real estate developer who often held large public meetings to interest potential investors in new projects, wondered if he could pick out those who would be most receptive to his approach before and after the meetings. Though I cautioned him that it was difficult for people standing around eating cheese and crackers to exude many obvious signals of interest, we did come up with clues that he found valuable.

Receptivity Signals

Look for one or more of these interest signs:

1. When you glance in a potential conversational partner's direction, he smiles, nods, or looks especially pleasant. Also, someone who hopes to speak with you may unconsciously mirror your stance or movement. One study of bar courtship found that single people who felt interested in meeting each other often held a drink or tapped to the music similarly.

2. While you are talking to someone else, she positions herself in nearby territory.

3. If you have approached someone near him, he hangs around instead of running for the cheese dip across the room.

4. If you are chatting your way around the room, you see her looking your way every so often.

5. He approaches you first—the clearest sign of interest in conversation.

To Increase Receptivity

1. Wait for or initiate a few nonverbal interchanges (smiles, nods) before you approach.

Note: Some people, ashamed to look too eager, actually look colder the more interested they are, so don't overinterpret lack of reciprocation.

2. Begin a conversation with someone both of you know—within his view.

3. Plan on having someone you both know introduce her.

Apart from all this scheming and sign reading, take the risk of initiating anyway. The most you have to lose is a decent conversation.

• Some People Can Begin Conversations Anywhere. Why Can't I?

It may have something to do with where they grew up. Remember Paul Hogan in *Crocodile Dundee*, throwing greetings everywhere when he arrived in New York City? Manhattanites were amazed or suspicious at his behavior, which was normal in Australian bush country.

Aside from regional differences, however, some folks do seem blessed with an extra dose of conversational confidence. If we look closely at the makeup of an outgoing individual, we usually find certain key beliefs and attitudes:

1. One principle is that *you needn't save friendliness for people in your inner circle*. People who easily start conversations generally take an interest in strangers they encounter in everyday life: the nanny pushing a carriage holding triplets, the bank teller sporting a great tan in the dead of winter, the teenager who seems proud of the green streak in her hair. Conversational openers stem naturally from their interest.

2. An even more important attitude is that *it's OK to say hi to anyone anywhere*—even to a stranger in the other corner of the elevator. Will the conversation necessarily go anyplace? Unlikely but possible. It would indeed be a wonderful world if everyone with whom we started a conversation became a soulmate or at least did more than grunt back.

3. On the real elevator of life, courageous conversers also know this: *Not everyone we want to talk to also wants to talk to us.* Think about it. Just as you send out reams of resumes in order to get your share of job interviews, good conversationalists increase their chances of finding a lover, pal, business connection, or pleasant repartee by starting many conversations—but they don't expect all of them to work out.

At my suggestion, my client Manny, a warm but shy physician, conducted an experiment while riding the train to work every day. His goal was to say hello to at least ten people a week and report the results to me. To his surprise more than half of the people he greeted proved willing to engage in a short conversation. The rest remained remote, but none were rude. His big news was that one attractive woman took his card and said she would call him to meet for lunch.

Manny's results sound right on target. About 10 percent of responses to conversational initiators will be positive. The rest will range from lack of interest to moderate engagement. Now ask yourself, is it worth it to take a chance at beginning conversation? Give it a try. Develop the mind-set of a courageous converser, and who knows what will come of your next elevator excursion?

• I Hate Small Talk

Is small talk really so small? Chitchat about unimportant matters provides warm-up time for more meaningful interaction. During small talk, shifts in several dimensions of interaction can occur—from discomfort to comfort, mistrust to trust, impersonal topics to personal ones. Then talkers turn to their real business.

Jay, an intense engineer who wanted to meet his soulmate, refused to make small talk. He insisted, "I like to walk up to a woman and say, 'I've been divorced three times, and I finally know myself well enough to sustain a close relationship.' " Unfortunately, he turned off more women than he turned on with his direct approach.

How to Make Your Peace With Small Talk

1. Appreciate small talk as a normal, necessary stage before a more meaningful exchange. Without small talk your style of interaction will seem rude or cold.

2. Use small-talk time to convey warmth and interest in your conversational partner. The content of what you are saying matters little. If someone makes an inane remark, it's fine to make an equally insipid comment to get the dance of conversation going. Make eye contact, wear a warm, involved expression, and nod your head to show interest.

3. After introductions, think about what you have in common with the other person to decide what to say. You will even have certain things in common with strangers. At a beach party, for example, there are the physical surroundings, the host and guests, the food, the music, and yes, the weather. Try a simple comment:

> "Incredible day!"
> "Have some avocado dip—it's scrumptious."

or a question:

> "Who's winning in volleyball?"
> "Are you another longtime friend of Patsy's?"

4. The small-talk phase is usually short. In business there should be a maximum of five minutes before getting to your real purpose. Allow the same amount of time in social situations before turning to the really interesting stuff. Whenever you're feeling frustrated with the degree of small talk, use a transition such as:

> "So what exactly is your role at ZYX?"
> "I'm really glad you invited me here to discuss your marketing plan."

(You wouldn't normally make such comments first thing.)

Remember: Don't worry about being clever. Just enter into the game of conversation, starting with the little moves necessary to get the game rolling smoothly.

• How Do I Get Someone to Open Up?

Mostly by not trying or prying. Like flowers, people blossom at different times. Your job is to create the right climate, the right conversational weather conditions, for building trust, which will nourish openness. Good communicators don't so much get people to open up as create the comfort necessary for others to want to share themselves. Here is how to create a climate for openness.

1. Don't come on too strong. Be a breeze, not a storm. People feel overwhelmed by someone who wants to know too much personal information too soon.

2. Let the person emerge at his or her own pace. Make your invitation to confide warm and generous, but optional. Allow your conversational partner to decide what and what not to say.

Some Good Openness Openers

Gentle prompts:

"If you would like to get into it, I'd love to hear about . . . [your sister's wedding, your opinion on the new tax law]."

"You mentioned an interest in [birds from Brazil, old jazz 78s]. If you feel like it, I'm interested in hearing more."

Not as gentle but still good prompts:

"Tell me a bit more about . . . [your stay with the family in France, your fear of bicycles]."

"It would be great to hear about . . . [your Peace Corps days, how you talked that guy out of jumping off the bridge]."

The Mr. or Ms. Availability prompt:

"If you ever feel like talking about it, I'd be more than happy to listen."

Open questions:

As their name suggests, the language of these questions usually leads to as little or as much openness as the person is ready for. They don't provoke a simple yes or no answer.

"How are things going with the promotion?" (Versus: "Do you like the promotion?")

"What kinds of winter sports are you into?" (Versus: "Do you like snowshoeing?")

"What do you think about aid to Central America?" (Versus: "Do you think our policy in Central America is working?")

Above all, *remember:* We can't get people to open up, but we can help them want to.

• I'm Never Sure Whether Someone Wants to Keep Talking to Me

Some of my socially anxious clients interpret anything short of 100 percent attention as a sign that the other person isn't interested: Roy, a systems analyst, said he knew Suzy was rejecting him because she sneezed during their last dinner date. Others don't readily see that their conversational partner would rather be on his way than spend another twenty or thirty minutes with them. The following tips should help you tune up your conversational radar.

A conversation has cooled when:

1. Your partner answers every question with two syllables or fewer (speech professionals call this "minimal response").

2. Your partner has already left the conversation with some part of his body; for example, his hand on the doorknob; her face toward you but body angled away, toward the exit; his gaze diverted upward, sideways, any way but at you.

3. Your partner is dropping frequent exit cues (comments that refer to a time and place without you):

> "My brother is calling from Tibet in ten minutes and I have to get home."

> "I really should say hi to the people in Ted's department."

> "Uh-oh, I'm already late for that meeting to plan the winter fund-raiser."

Once you catch these "gotta go" signals, get going. Regardless of your wish to fan the conversation back to life, let it die with dignity by saying good-bye first. See "I Don't Know How to End a Conversation" (page 58) for painless sign-off strategies.

• I Don't Know How to Change the Subject When I'm Bored to Tears

If you like the person you are speaking with but not the subject, your goal is to strategically shift the conversation into more appealing territory. Try these conversation detours:

1. *Bridging.* Bring up a topic that was mentioned earlier or one that you know you have in common. For example: "You said that you'll be spending a month in Japan. I'd love to hear about your travel plans."

2. *Redirecting.* Express appreciation for the present topic but then immediately shift to one that interests you. "It's super that you know so much about kangaroos. I was wondering, though, if I could get your input on how long it will take to get our new phone system working."

3. *Switching tracks.* This requires quick thinking. Pick up on a key word or phrase from what the other person is saying and offer a question or comment that leads away from Yawnsville. "Speaking of balmy weather, did I tell you that I'll be going to Nashville in May?"

4. *Roadblock.* If all else fails, try the most direct method of foiling a bore: Offer a polite but direct statement that shows your lack of interest. Try these handy phrases for starters:

"You know, I'm not really into that [collecting stamps from Lapland]. Do you mind if we change the subject?"

"Frankly, I have a thing against talking about that [the weather] for so long. Can we talk about something else?"

• I Can Never Think of Anything Clever to Say

Since conversation is the principal way we make everyday human contact, every high school should require Conversation I and Advanced Conversation. Still, it is never too late to become a conversation connoisseur.

1. Pick three people (in your life or the media) whose conversational skills you admire. Try to come up with at least three specific traits they have that make their conversation especially appealing. Examples:

> My favorite, Johnny Carson, adapts well to many different personalities, laughs at himself, always remains calm, and is a good-natured tease.
>
> My aunt Ann makes daily life events interesting, talks just the right amount, and adds a twinge of sarcasm that keeps you interested.

2. Next, know yourself. You want to develop your own conversational style, not a pale imitation of Regis Philbin's. To get started, look at this list of effective conversational types and pick two or three that most resemble you at your best.

> *Storyteller:* loves to associate a topic of conversation with a personal experience. Usually a people person with a good memory.
>
> Favorite line: "That reminds me of the time . . ."
>
> Famous storytellers: Jack Benny, Bob Hope, your grandfather.
>
> *Feeler:* focuses on emotions and opinions. Can be a dramatic or sensitive listener and knows how to draw you out and hold your interest.

Favorite line: "How awful [wonderful, and so forth]."
Famous feelers: Barbara Walters, Oprah Winfrey.

Thinker: has a gift for opinions, interpretation, and seeing the larger picture.
Favorite line: "Another way to look at it is . . ."
Famous thinkers: Dick Cavett, David Frost.

Prober: gets the other person to talk. The other person finds himself the center of attention and may later describe the prober as fascinating.
Favorite line: "Tell me about . . ."
Famous probers: Ted Koppel, your shrink.

Chatterer: keeps up the flow of conversation with anyone breathing. Chatterers like to keep the music going, though they don't necessarily care about the words.
Favorite line: "Oh, did you hear about . . ."
Famous chatterers: Edith Bunker, Zsa Zsa Gabor.

Creative converser: says things most people would never think of. Always a unique angle.
Characteristic line: "If you could be a fruit, which would you be?"
Famous creative conversers: Lily Tomlin, Robin Williams.

Pick two or three styles that are the most comfortable for you and seek out opportunities to develop these in your conversation for the next month.

3. No matter what your style, *remember: To be an interesting conversationalist, be an interesting person!* You'll find plenty of interesting things to speak about if you read a daily newspaper and a weekly general-interest magazine. Your knowledge base ought to extend beyond your neighborhood and your professional specialty. Only a small percentage of the U.S. population

has much to say about prestressed concrete, and not everybody you meet is going to care about the Mets. For an important informal occasion you might even preplan two or three topics to bring up.

4. Keep in mind that you're trying to bring out your best self, not a fake self. Whenever you try something new, such as offering a controversial opinion or telling a dumb joke, you may feel funny because of the newness. Ask yourself, Is this me? Is this a me I'd like to keep? If the answer is yes, then it's a go—conversationally speaking.

• My Conversations Always Seem to Die

Conversation is best thought of as a game where partners take turns holding the conversational ball. Fittingly, communication scientists even use the term "conversational volley." Good conversationalists are not so much experts on different topics—though it helps to be aware of what's going on in the world—as good game players. They know and use the moves that keep themselves and others out of the conversational dead zone.

To Keep the Conversational Ball Going

1. *Start a new round.* Introduce a new topic after a lull. This is easier if you approach any important conversation with at least three topics you could raise as comments or questions:

> "I saw a fantastic old film last night."
> "What do you think about colorized films?"

Handy starter phrases:

> "I wanted to ask you about . . ."
> "Did I tell you about . . ."
> "Oh, I just remembered . . ."
> "That reminds me of . . ."
> "I can't believe what I heard about . . ."
> "There's something I wanted to share with you . . ."
> "Oh, listen to this . . ."

2. *Expand.* Try to stretch the topic at hand by adding a different dimension to what was just said. If you've been chatting about a snowstorm, for instance, consider these levels of play:

Facts and information: "They're saying we should expect five more inches this weekend."

Opinions: "Don't you think the town is doing a great job keeping the roads open?"

Examples and experiences: "Until I started skiing I stayed inside all winter. Now I look forward to a big storm."

3. *Pick up a dropped topic.* Return to information that came up earlier. This requires good listening all along in order to keep in mind what conversational tidbits you can toss back in for another volley.

> "You mentioned you're interested in building your own home. Do you have a site picked out yet?"

4. *Allow time out.* Comfortable conversations include some silent periods. Tolerate a time out by counting to ten in your head the next time there is silence. You may be surprised to find that your partner has casually and effectively started the volley going again.

**In the game of conversation,
give the other guy three chances
to return the ball.
If he doesn't, he's out!**

• I Don't Know How to End a Conversation

Time wasted on business calls that go on too long runs into the millions, if not billions, of hours every year, and social encounters that seem to go on forever plague just as many of us. Penelope, a participant in one of my conversation workshops, told me that she had given up going to parties because inevitably some great monologist would corner her until she was desperate for a polite way to go on to someone else. She would nod glassy-eyed until the tiresome fellow got tired of her or the party broke up.

Conversations keep on going because you keep giving off signals that you would like the conversation to continue. Switch your signals and you will be able to end any conversation for any reason at any time.

To Switch Signals

First, stop giving these *green lights:*

1. Saying uh-huh and mm-hmm (these little sounds are appropriately called "encouragers").
2. Nodding your head, looking eager, interested, fascinated, or inquisitive.
3. Introducing a new topic, adding a comment, questioning or complimenting.

   In other words, *SHHHH!*

Next, these *red lights* will signal that you're ready to stop:

1. Moving backward or sideways as if you're starting a getaway.
2. Looking at anything but your conversational partner's face.

3. Using the *Plus Arrow Plus* technique for your exiting lines.

The *Plus Arrow Plus* technique is a simple strategy that allows you to leave with tact and grace:

The *Plus* +*:* Say something positive about the person or the conversation.

"It was good talking to you about desktop publishing."

The *Arrow* →*:* Clearly state what you need to do.

"I need to say hi to a couple of other people here."

The *Plus* + again: Add one more positive comment and leave.

"It was a pleasure meeting you. Bye."

You needn't ever feel trapped. Get rid of your *green lights*, set up some *red lights*, remember *Plus Arrow Plus*, and you'll be free again.

• I'm a "Toucher," but I Know It Turns Some People Off

Congratulations for recognizing that some people prefer a hands-off policy—many touchers think that everyone loves to be touched as much as they do. Actually, whether you should touch or not depends on the situation, the relationship, and the personalities.

Kathy, an energetic manager in law enforcement, was accustomed to giving colleagues she hadn't seen in a long time what she thought of as a "business hello"—a peck on the cheek. She was shocked when she overheard a colleague refer to her mockingly as "Miss Kiss." Since she wanted to be known for her law enforcement expertise, not what she did with her lips, we worked on having her achieve the "right touch."

To Get the Right Touch

1. Remember that other people may not be as touchable as you are.

2. Back off at any of these signs of withdrawal: your conversational partner moves away, hunches, looks distracted, or puts a barrier between the two of you. Most people don't like to seem "touchy" about being touched, so recognize the subtle hints.

3. Look for evidence of reciprocation. Over time, someone should be touching you as much as you're touching him. If not, he may not appreciate your pats and taps. When in doubt, restrain yourself.

4. Watch the degree of force you use. A hard backslap may not be felt as the friendly gesture you intend it to be.

5. Be especially sensitive to the relationship between power and touch. The person with the higher status in a situation may

unconsciously be touching more, and the lower-status person may feel uncomfortable about reciprocating or rebuffing him. You may *think* you're touching to be friendly but examine your motives. Could it be to show one-upmanship?

6. Use special caution in business situations with the opposite sex, particularly when you're in a superior/inferior relationship. You may think you're giving the administrative assistant a prolonged hug of appreciation, but she may consider it sexual harassment and march upstairs to file a complaint.

To Control Your Urge to Reach Out and Touch

1. Observe your usual touch patterns. Notice who you touch, how, and when.

2. Experiment with touching less with people who seem turned off. Carry folders or clipboards if you need to keep your hands in check.

3. If that tactile sensation reassures you, touch a desk or a chair while making a point.

4. Visualization can help. Imagine that your touch will feel like an electric shock. Extreme, I know, but it will help you keep your distance.

• How Do I Approach a Famous Person Without Making a Fool of Myself?

You're a brave soul even to think about approaching an idol, since most of us tend to keep a respectful distance. One study showed that in a large room we leave at least twenty feet between ourselves and the famous face. But since celebrity is based on admiration, famous folks do often respond well to fans who know how to fawn appropriately. Of course, the reception you get depends on when and where you approach as much as what you say.

Interaction with your idol is *not* recommended:

1. While she is just biting into a burger. Let Cher chew in peace.
2. While she's rushing to catch a plane.
3. When he's walking down the street with a hat pulled low over his face, trying not to be noticed.
4. At the dentist's in the middle of a root canal.
5. In the next toilet stall. Yes, even Prince Charles goes.

More successful encounters can be expected at such occasions as public appearances, book signings, fund-raisers, before or after a show, or if you happen to spot your hero doing nothing and looking bored. Don't expect Selleck or Madonna to follow you into the nearest bar for a three-hour tête-à-tête, but if he or she has time and you smile in just the right way, who knows?

Now, what to say? Here are two different strategies.

The Gush Rush

1. Gush if you must, but don't screech, and keep it brief.

> "It's such a thrill for me . . ."
> "I'm so excited to be . . ."

2. Explain what makes you gush.

> ". . . 'cause your songs got me through all the hard times in my life."
> ". . . I'm mesmerized by you every Thursday at nine."

3. Close by referring to the future (no, not yours with hers or his truly).

> "I'll be looking forward to your next movie."
> "I'll be watching for you on the 'Rollin' Rodeo Show.' "

4. Finally, get your last close-up look. Gaze a second more at the famous facade, and unless you're asked to take a moonlight cruise, just the two of you, scram. Your brush with greatness has left a positive impression if only for a brief moment in time.

The Class Harass

1. You cool, sophisticated fans might do better with a slicker approach. Saunter up as if you have just recognized your arch-rival from high school. Hold out your hand. Act as if you are just as important as Mr. or Ms. Greatness.

> "Mr. Kissinger, how nice to see you."
> "Ms. Steinem, what a pleasure."

2. Say something provocative—the more specific the better.

> "I really couldn't agree with what you said last month on *Meet the Press*. Doesn't the United States need to be morally above reproach?"
> "Are you coming out with another book anytime soon? American women need to be shaken out of their complacency."

3. If you have managed to say something they haven't heard before, kudos! Drink in every word of the reply so you can tell your children and grandchildren. If you get a blank look or a glare, though, smile or wave good-bye and exit quickly.

> "Well, take care . . ."

....

Telephone Hangups

• Is There a Best Way to Answer the Telephone at Work?

If you are in business, it's critical to put a lot of thought into how you greet callers. During those first few seconds, a caller sizes up your approachability, mood, professionalism—and may even get a mental picture of what you look like. On the practical side, your first few words let the caller know he has reached the right person or firm—that is, if your articulation is clear and you're not talking a mile a minute.

Once in a telephone skills workshop a client named Larry complained that when he answered the phone with "Saint Paul's Hospital," people would often ask, "Is this Saint Paul's Hospital?" As an experiment, the day after the program, I called and heard an utterance that sounded something like "Pa's Hospital." Kind of folksy but not exactly good public relations for Saint Paul's. Larry, like many people who speak for their organizations, needed to become more conscious of the dos and don'ts for greeting the public.

Greeting Dos and Don'ts

Don't:
- Speak too fast or mumbly. (See "People Often Ask Me to Repeat Myself," page 8.)
- Assume the caller knows who you are.
- Use a mile-long greeting. The other day I heard, "Welcome to the wonderful world of travel at Parker's World-wide Bureau. This is Gerda Litnick. How may I help you or direct your call?" Enough already!
- Talk to your coworkers as you pick up the phone. Recently my colleague dialed a prestigious university and heard, "That's what you call a hot date! [Pause] Good morning, Office of Personnel, may I help you?"

Do:

- Practice using close-to-perfect speech and voice habits in your greeting. It is essential to sound positive and warm. Tape yourself to judge whether the sound of your voice would give callers a good feeling.
- Say *all* the syllables in your name and the name of your company. I know you've said it 1,112 times in the past hour, but the guy on the other end needs confirmation that he's reached you, not the local dump.
- Find a short, friendly greeting that sets the right mood. Your hello should include most or all of these parts:

1. "Hello" (not "Hi" in business) or "Good morning," and so forth.

2. Name of your firm or department, or both: "Courteous Collection Company, Human Resources."

3. Your name: "This is Carly Brannigan."

4. Offer of assistance: "How may I help you?" or "How may I direct your call?"

During your weekly phone experiences, note positive and negative examples of phone greetings, and add your own dos and don'ts to this list.

• How Do I Get Past the Secretary?

First, change your attitude. Why try to get past a secretary? Better to try to get through to her by acknowledging her importance and value. Secretaries are not answering machines, they're front-line people who often make important decisions about who will get in and who will get lost. A recent study indicated that we don't get through to the person we attempt to call 75 percent of the time. So in your plan to get the head honcho's ear, don't ignore the honcho's right-hand person.

Jamie, a free-lance fashion designer, was rarely able to get any appointments with industry executives despite good references. I observed her making a sample call to a corporate vice president she had been trying to connect with in three previous calls. Embarrassed to leave one more message, she told the VP's assistant that she would call back. Nothing rude about that, but remaining anonymous to a potential ally is not the way to get ahead.

How to Get Through to a Secretary

1. Sound pleased to speak with her. Leave a message in an upbeat tone of voice, use personable language, and add a personal thanks.

No: "Just tell him that Karen Reese called again."
Yes: "This is Karen Reese. I would appreciate it if you'd leave a message for Mr. Stern to give me a call when he can after three. Thanks so much for your help."

2. Get on a first-name basis. By the second or third call it's helpful to use the secretary's name when leaving a message as a step in building a more personal relationship.

If she's told you her name:

"You've been so helpful. I really appreciate it, Pam."
"Thanks for taking such a lengthy message, Pam."

If a name hasn't been offered, tactfully ask:

"Thanks so much for your help in getting these messages to Mr. Stern. And your name is—?"

3. Offer sincere and specific compliments. Many administrative personnel are overworked and underpraised. Your thoughtfulness will stand out, and you'll end up more memorable to the secretary and, eventually, to the boss.

"You know, you have a wonderful phone voice."
"Most people don't pronounce my name correctly the first time—thanks."

4. Enlist the secretary as a helpmate. People like to be needed, especially people who have chosen a job where they provide service to others. Ask for a small favor that only she can help you with.

"I wonder if you could help me out, Pam. Tomorrow's my deadline. Would it be possible to set up a phone appointment with Mr. Stern before five today?"
"I know Mr. Stern is busy and can't see everyone, but I'm convinced that he'll be glad to know about our special offer for ad space in the special trade show issue of our magazine. Do you think he has five minutes in his schedule anytime this week?"

Remember: Polite persistence usually succeeds.

• What's the Nicest Way to Put Someone on Hold?

Callers vary in their reaction to being put on hold. Some view it as a minor inconvenience, like having to wait in line at the bank, while others experience it as a slap in the face: "They want my business and treat me like this!" Unfortunately, putting people on hold is often a necessity.

Though it is not easy to find a polite way of temporarily ignoring someone, you can make the hold as painless as possible by applying in just three steps the same principles of courtesy you would use in a face-to-face encounter.

Polite Holding Patterns

1. Give the caller a reason for the hold. If she were in your living room, you wouldn't dart away for no reason. For example:

> "I need to get your file."
> "Let me see if Mr. Meng is available."
> "I'll be happy to ask Ms. Neal."

If you expect the hold to last a minute or more, it's best to ask if you can call her back. One busy executive refuses to wait on hold even forty-five seconds. He watches his second hand and hangs up when half a minute has passed.

2. Ask the caller if she would *mind* holding.

> "Would you mind holding?"
> "Would you care to hold?"
> "Could you stay on the line for ten minutes and listen to our recording?" (Just kidding on that one.)

Better yet, ask the caller if she prefers to hold or to leave a message. Any time you offer a choice, you treat the caller more considerately.

3. When you return, thank the caller for waiting.

> "Thanks for waiting."
> "Sorry for the delay."

Wouldn't you say something similar if you were talking to someone in your kitchen and got up to answer the doorbell or the phone?

The same principles apply to call-waiting, which is increasingly popular for home phones. Some people find it annoying to be interrupted by a click and then left hanging while the person they were talking with sees who else wants to talk to them. They will be less apt to take offense if you give a reason for putting them on hold, make the wait as brief as possible, and acknowledge the delay when you come back.

> [Click] "That might be my son. Hang on, I'll be right back. . . . Sorry, it was a wrong number. You were telling me about your daughter's friend who wears chains?"
>
> [Click] "Oh, I'm expecting a call from my publisher. Can you hang on for a minute? . . . Thanks, Dan. It *is* my publisher. Can I call you back in half an hour?"

Call-waiting appeals to people who hate missing someone who is trying to reach them. But if you habitually keep first callers waiting while you chat on and on with someone else, or end conversations for another call without a polite excuse, you're sending a message even worse than that impersonal, old-fashioned busy signal.

• My Coworkers Bother Me When I'm on the Telephone

Many clients who work in an open office where people freely walk in, out, and around voice this complaint. Instead of blaming the problem on inconsiderate coworkers, however, it is better to focus on changes you can make in your own behavior to forestall the problem. By broadcasting "Do Not Disturb" loud and clear, you *can* stop people from asking you to carry on two conversations with only one mouth.

To broadcast "Do not disturb—I'm on the telephone":

1. *Signal.* Put up a flag or sign that indicates you're on the phone and can't be bothered. Or use an uplifted finger (the index one will do) to let your office mate know that she'll have to wait.

2. *Ignore.* Focus on your phone call, not the goings-on around you. Since people are more likely to interrupt if they can establish eye contact with you, keep your gaze on something inanimate, like the wall or your coffee cup. Your body position and posture should indicate that you're busy and involved, not bored and hoping for a better conversation to come along. One client who used to smile at passersby turned her chair so they would see her back instead of her face.

3. *Sensitize.* Discuss the problem with each phone intruder privately. Let him know you'd be glad to talk to him when you're not on the phone. If you're being interrupted because you're always on the phone and coworkers sometimes really do need prompt attention, then ask them to pass you a note so you can end or interrupt your call yourself.

4. *Formalize.* Set up regular hours when you don't take calls so you can attend to your in-person interactions.

• What If I Have to Get Someone's Attention in Thirty Seconds?

Helping your listener recognize in thirty seconds or less the benefits of what you, your product, or your service can offer is a stiff communication challenge. To prevent a prospect from slipping away, hook your callee by appealing to his needs, wants, or interests—without spreading it on too thick. From the listener's perspective, if the first thirty seconds are appealing enough, he'll be glad to let your pitch take even more of his precious time.

Lou, a professional golfer, was rounding up investors for an innovative golf school he planned to open and was puzzled by the poor response to his telephone contacts with prospective backers. Not long into his opening remarks he would often hear, "Sorry, not interested" and then a dial tone. When I listened to him make a sample call in my office, I could immediately tell why people didn't want to hear him out. After saying "hello," Lou launched into a canned spiel, remotely and mechanically delivered. He might as well have been a computer calling! But after working on the strategies that follow, Lou told me that his telephone score was reaching par, with many more potential investors agreeing to set up a meeting.

Tips for Quick Ear-Catching

Don't:
- assume the person won't be interested
- deliver a canned or overly planned presentation
- do all the talking

Do:
- assume you have something worthwhile to say

- plan remarks that are unique to the person on the line
- use *The Three I's* for fast results:

Introduce yourself and your company briefly: "This is Lou Kincaid, president of the Champions Golf School."

Interest your callee by commenting on how he could connect with the purpose of your call: "Before we open our program, I'd like to provide you with some excellent investment opportunities as well as benefit from your marketing experience."

Involve your callee by asking questions that enhance interaction and comfort. Here are a few question types:

1. *Leading question*—the kind that usually will receive a positive answer: "Do you think the idea of a golf school will appeal to many golfers?"

2. *Open-door question*—designed to get your callee talking: "Harry, I understand that you went to a golf school in Florida. How did you like the experience?"

3. *Assessment question*—helps you assess a client's need or interest level: "What type of projects are you interested in becoming involved with, investment-wise?"

4. *Opinion question*—shows the callee you value his perspective. People like being thought of as an expert: "Harry, what's your judgment? How do you think weekend programs for advanced golfers would go over?"

If your listener responds in complete sentences (versus grunting), it's a good sign that you've won that person's attention.

• I Hate Calling People I Don't Know

Not knowing how we'll be greeted and treated by someone we need to call scares many of us. When a job requires us to generate a large volume of calls and with that a large volume of rejections, it's more comfortable to stare at the telephone than pick it up.

Brenda, a food industry salesperson who had to call dozens of new potential customers every week, suffered from what has been labeled "call reluctance"—the fear of being treated like a pesky rodent. To avoid hearing that foreboding dial tone, she would do anything, from balancing her checkbook to emptying her colleagues' wastebaskets. Worried that she would not make it in sales, Brenda came to see me in hopes of salvaging her relationship with the telephone—and her self-confidence.

The Cure for Phonophobia

1. Remember that even if the worst happens and your callee insults or hangs up on you, the rejection hurts for only an instant. Rarely will you ever need to speak with the rejecter again.

2. Set a goal of a certain number of calls to make each hour and each day. Promise yourself a goodie as a reward at the end of the week.

> "I made thirty-five calls this week, so I'll get myself a subscription to *Sports Illustrated*."

Reward yourself in smaller ways for smaller chunks of completed calls.

> "I'll get something from the juice machine after these five calls, not before . . ."

3. Decide on a specific desired outcome for each call to reduce pressure on yourself. Use these words:

> "I will be satisfied if . . . I just introduce myself."
> . . . I let her know I'll be sending my brochure."
> . . . he orders some samples."

4. Plan a strategy for getting your point across. This formula, for instance, often works:

(1) Introduce yourself and your company
(2) Relate what you are offering to their needs
(3) Ask a question to get involvement
(4) Describe what you have to offer
(5) End by describing what you will do next

(1) "Hi, I'm Mark Washington from the Comedy Hour Club. (2) I know your firm is interested in creative business ideas, and I'd like to share a bit about our franchise with you. (3) Are you familiar with the Comedy Hour Club in Cleveland? So you've heard mixed reviews . . . (4) Recently we've upgraded the quality of our sound equipment and light snacks to outdo our main competition, The Funny Zone. (5) I'd like to send you our material and then perhaps we can meet when I'm in Peoria next month."

5. Tack this saying up above your phone:

> Stop bawling, start calling
> Stop balking, start talking
> Stop fretting, start getting
> Stop filing, start dialing—
> Not tomorrow, not after lunch, not when you feel like it, NOW!

• I Always Forget What I Wanted to Say

There's only one thing worse than forgetting what you called about and that's forgetting *who* you called. Short of putting yourself in an isolation tank, it's hard to avoid being distracted between the time you dial the number and the time you finally speak to What's-his-name. During the ten seconds to ten (heaven help us) minutes it takes for the person to come on the line, your brain naturally gets involved in other interests: *People* magazine, your hangnail, what your next five calls will be about, the meaning of life . . . Then zing! Mr. Whozits finally says hello, and after all that waiting, you're speechless.

To avoid telephone amnesia, remember *T-E-L:*

Tune in to the purpose of your call and tune out distractions. Have only papers pertaining to the task at hand in front of you. If this were a face-to-face meeting, you would not be reading the newspaper while sitting across the desk from Mr. Whozits, would you?

Expect one solid outcome from the call: a future meeting for lunch, a pleasant social chat, a million dollars in orders, whatever. Without any idea of what you want from the call, you might as well say, "Sorry, wrong number," and hang up.

List key points you want to make in note form before you place the call. Nothing fancy, just key words that will jog your memory no matter what universe you're in when your party finally comes on. Don't forget to list points you want to make in the opening small talk (ask about vacation, the new baby) and parting words (see you at the Chamber of Commerce meeting in November). If you're the organized type, check off each point as the call moves along.

• Telephone Tag Is Driving Me Nuts

Telephone tag is a simple game to learn but frustrating to play. You and your tag partner never speak but leave each other endless messages. Though you can't control when someone else is available, you can minimize your role in this frustrating chase.

How to Bring the Game to a Close

1. If you are reaching each other's machines, include in your message three times when you can definitely be reached.

2. Ask the secretary for a specific time that would be good for calling back. At the end of the conversation, reconfirm: "So I'll be calling Mr. Juarez at one tomorrow. I'll write it in my book."

3. Set regular hours when you will be in to receive calls. For your most important elusive callers, have your secretary set up phone appointments.

4. Try asking if your tag partner comes in early or stays late. These could be better times for reaching him.

5. If you're really interested in speaking and you're not far from each other, set up an in-person appointment through the secretary.

6. Cozy up to the secretary by asking, "Can you help me out? Pete and I have been trying to catch each other since Wednesday. What can you suggest so we can speak today?"

7. Leave a humorous message, such as, "The suspense is killing me!" or "It's been a pleasure getting to know your secretary." The lightness might make you more memorable and worth trying to find.

8. If you don't want your tag partner to get as frustrated as you are, make it a game of one. Tell the secretary that you'll try again and Millie needn't call you since you'll be in conference most of the day.

• I Hate Leaving Messages on Answering Machines

Answermachinephobia is a modern-day hangup. Some of us are spooked by the idea of a permanent record of our voices, while others can't abide talking to a machine—it doesn't seem the human thing to do. Perhaps the most reasonable excuse for hanging up without leaving a message is fear of saying something stupid you can't erase.

Joe, a building contractor, left a message with a potential client finalizing fees for a custom-built home. After the beep he said: "Mr. and Mrs. Davine, here are the start-up figures: eight thousand for labor, two thousand for truck rentals, and three thousand for materials. Get back to me." That evening, Mrs. Davine called Joe in a tizzy, concerned that something was very wrong with the design of their house. "What makes you say that?" asked Joe. She replied, "At the end of the tape you mumbled, 'I hate dealing with this. It's the worst thing I have to do.'" Indeed, not realizing the tape was still running, he *had* said that, only he was talking to himself about the answering machine, not their custom-built home.

Every phone user nowadays needs to know these dos and don'ts for talking to a tape:

Do:

1. If you know there is a chance a machine will answer, decide beforehand whether you'll leave a message and the main points you'll make.
2. Act conversational, not stiff or formal. Eventually a person, not the machine, will listen to you.
3. Say important numbers or addresses slowly and clearly. Even better, repeat them so the recipient of the message won't have to rewind the tape and play it back a second time.

4. See the machine as a communication opportunity. Call a friend or colleague just to say thank you, I appreciate you, miss you, or can't live without you. When he or she gets home and listens to other people's hangups, mumbles, and miscommunications, your message will definitely be heard.

Don't:
1. Go on forever. The owner of the machine will be listening for messages, not monologues.
2. Reveal any secret or personal information. Machines are often played back in front of others. Joyce, a friend of mine, found out about her own surprise birthday party by overhearing on a friend's machine, "I'll see you at Joyce's on Friday night."
3. Talk to yourself or others before or after the message. Remember what happened to Joe. The tape catches everything you say.
4. Chew or crack gum, clear your throat, or stand next to a blaring TV or radio—unless you want to create a sloppy impression.

··········

Nerves

• Is There a Quick Way to Get Rid of Nervousness?

It would be great if there were a confidence capsule we could crunch in the morning with our corn flakes. Until science comes to the rescue, we'll have to be content with just reducing nervousness. Think of degrees of nervousness along a continuum from 1 to 10, where 1 represents minimum jitters—total relaxation, the way you might feel lying on a warm beach with your toes curled into the sand. Ten represents maximum terror—fear so dreadful that it's impossible for you to concentrate or talk coherently. For an important speaking occasion, we would not expect a day at the beach, nor could we do the job when petrified. The controlled nervousness zone, where it's possible to perform decently despite the shakes, is higher than you might expect—6 to 8.

Stephen, an office manager for a real estate firm, got the willies every time he had to give orders at a staff meeting. He hated playing the heavy. To help him control his fear, I shared with him the advice my father had offered to help me overcome my fear of driving on highways. I was driving for the first time on the Garden State Parkway, and as we approached the first toll booth, Dad said, "Put your foot on the brake." Guess what? The car stopped! I was rather in awe of the newfound power of my foot. My father looked at me and said, "Right now you feel as if it's controlling you. Soon you'll be controlling it." Years later, when I began working with people who were terrified of speaking, I remembered that lesson and developed the quickest, easiest stress reduction exercise you'll ever find. Using this technique, Stephen brought his anxiety down one notch on the scale at each meeting until it settled comfortably at 6.

The Pick-a-Tic Technique

That's right—choose your own nervous habit! This exercise helps you decide *how* you'll be nervous. Rather than having your body go haywire, you will exercise some conscious control over how your body will react. Simply squeeze together your thumb and middle finger for three seconds and slowly let go.

Do this as often as you need to in a stressful situation. You can also accompany the squeeze with inhaling and the release of the squeeze with exhaling.

Practice in all sorts of situations, such as dealing with irksome situations (waiting in line at the post office, trying to convince the hotel clerk that you really do need working light bulbs in your room) before trying it with full-scale stressors. The beauty of *Pick-a-tic* is that it's quite invisible if you position the squeezing fingers out of sight. It is ideal for controlling nervousness right before their very eyes!

• I Can't Sleep or Eat for Days Before an Upcoming Talk

Speech anxiety can be all-consuming, so let's tackle it head-on. First let's figure out what you're worried about. What exactly are you afraid may happen? What are some of the thoughts accompanying your anxiety? Once you identify the specific triggers for your fear, you can confront them.

Janet started worrying, weeks before a presentation, about not knowing the answers to questions from the audience. When I asked what would be so terrible about that, she replied with certainty, "I'd be humiliated and lose all credibility!" I helped her to see that that wouldn't necessarily happen. So long as she basically knew her material, not knowing the answer to one or two questions would not be a calamity. Offering to find the answer for the questioner would, in fact, enhance her professionalism. In addition, Janet gained confidence and a sense of control by anticipating the most likely questions the audience might ask and preparing responses to them in advance.

To cut worry down to size, follow these four steps:

1. *Identify.* As Janet did, say exactly what you are frightened of. Don't blame yourself for being silly. If you're afraid of someone releasing snakes in the room during your lecture, that fear is real to you and deserves respect. Here are some fears clients often share with me:

> People will notice I'm nervous.
> I'll go blank.
> They'll ask me a question I can't answer.
> People will laugh when I'm not trying to be funny.

Also identify what you think the consequences of that fear may be. For example:

If I go blank, people will think I'm incompetent and I'll be fired.

2. *Debate.* To diminish the hold of the fear, take a rational look at your underlying thoughts and beliefs. Is it absolutely, necessarily, 100 percent certain that the scenario terrorizing you would have the consequences you fear? Often another person can help you be more objective here. Write down your fear and then debate it, like this:

Worry: If I drop my notes, I'll make a fool of myself and lose my job.

Debate: Everyone drops notes once in a while, and they don't usually lose their job.

The audience may feel uncomfortable and embarrassed for me, but this will last only a few moments, and they won't decide I'm a fool.

I can drop my notes and still make a good impression on the audience if I handle the flub with poise.

3. *Counteract.* Choose the most persuasive items in your debate and repeat them to yourself several times a day. Be sure to do this when an unhelpful thought creeps into your mind and particularly during final preparations for your talk. These "success sentences" will become more powerful than your stressful sentences.

4. *Troubleshoot.* Formulate practical actions you can take to reduce the likelihood of your feared scenario and its feared consequences:

If I go blank, I'll take ten seconds to look calmly at my notes, reorganize my thoughts, and then continue.

To reinforce these coping strategies, close your eyes and visualize things going wrong and your handling it calmly several times a day the week before a talk.

Now let's put it all together with an example:

Worry:

If I make one mistake, I'll blow the whole thing and lose the Firestein account.

Success thoughts:

I might even make several mistakes, but they won't matter so long as I'm on the right track most of the time.

I don't have to be perfect. A couple of mistakes will help me look more human.

I have the ability to correct whatever I need to correct and move on.

Firestein isn't going to hold one little mistake against me when I'm generally well prepared and competent.

I can make a mistake and still do well. Look at Johnny Carson—he goofs in his monologues but never takes it very seriously.

Practical actions:

I'll rehearse the presentation thoroughly to troubleshoot the tough spots.

I'll prevent getting my numbers mixed up by preparing handouts with the most important figures.

I'll watch TV newscasters and notice how many mistakes they make and yet they're still popular.

Wouldn't it be wonderful if we each had a chorus following us around: Nothing to worry about, Myrna. Everything you say is a pearl of wisdom, Myrna. You're looking fine, Myrna. You'll go straight to the top, Myrna. In truth, we each have to be our own confidence chorus. It takes introspection and practice, but a realistic and even positive attitude toward yourself as a speaker is certainly achievable.

• If Only I Could Relax . . .

Nervousness about speaking has two major components, both of which may seem to be outside your control. First, there is the physical aspect, stemming from the body's instinctive reaction to danger (to many of us, an audience is as dangerous as a bear charging our way). In the so-called fight-or-flight response, adrenaline is released, the heart beats faster, the blood goes to vital organs rather than to extremities ("cold feet"), and you may sweat, blush, and so forth. This is how the body gears up for an emergency. Second, there is the psychological response to a feared event, which can provoke, maintain, and worsen the physical responses. You may forget your company's name, feel disconnected from your body, and be besieged by panicky thoughts like "What on earth am I doing here?" or "I've botched it, my career is ruined."

It's not unusual to be terrified before speaking to an audience. On the contrary, in poll after poll, public speaking turns up in the Fear Hall of Fame. Most Americans rate speaking in front of a group as more frightening than heights, insects, and even death. Fortunately, this ordeal can be turned into a manageable challenge, using *The Three Cs:*

Comfort: things you can do to feel more physically normal. You'll remember that comfort was also discussed in "Is There a Quick Way to Get Rid of Nervousness?" (page 85).

Confidence: ways of thinking that decrease rather than increase nervousness. See "I Can't Sleep or Eat for Days Before an Upcoming Talk" (page 87) for strategies to counteract stressful thoughts.

Contact: strategies for extending yourself to the audience instead of being a speech robot. The tips in "How Do I Warm Up the Audience?" (page 124) and "How Do I Get Audience Participation?" (page 136) will help you feel less of a stranger to yourself in front of initially blank faces.

Increasing Your Comfort in Front
of a Group

1. *Stress-control breathing.* Your goal is to feel a sense of control over the physical reactions you're experiencing, keeping in mind that physical changes are normal. While it's hard to control your heartbeat or blood pressure, you can control, to a certain extent, the way you breathe. To test where your breathing is focused, put one hand on your stomach and the other on your chest. Under stress, the center of your breathing tends to move from your abdomen to your upper chest, leaving you with a smaller supply of air. With stressed breathing, in contrast, your chest and shoulders rise, and you feel out of breath. With stress-control breathing, you will feel more movement on your stomach than on your chest.

Learn stress-control breathing in two stages:

Stage one. Inhale air, and your abdomen goes out. Exhale air and your abdomen goes in. Simple, isn't it?

Stage two. Insert a lulling word such as *calm* or *relax* or a personal mantra in the stage-one formula, as follows: "Inhale *calm*, abdomen out, exhale *calm*, abdomen in." Say this to yourself while following the instructions. Go slowly. Each inhalation and exhalation of stress-control breathing takes about three to five seconds.

Long before you're scheduled to speak, practice stress-control breathing, first when you feel relaxed, then in semistressful situations such as talking to an annoying caller, and finally on semistressful occasions where you need to speak in front of people but are not the star speaker.

At your actual speaking event, while you're waiting for your turn, you can practice the above sequence, even putting your hand on your abdomen to notice how you're doing. After you've been called to the podium, you can focus on breathing once more while you're arranging your things and getting ready to begin. Take it slowly! Stress-control breathing helps you feel centered and inwardly calm.

2. *"The wave."* Under stress, your breathing and your voice can get uncoordinated. Unless you coordinate beginning to exhale and beginning to speak, you'll have trouble getting the words out and your nervousness will compound. Fortunately, it's not difficult to get your voice and breathing into harmony.

Picture a wave, with the rise from a trough representing inhalation and the fall from the crest representing exhalation. You want to start speaking at the crest of the wave, when you have the maximum amount of air in your system, so you don't waste breath or run out of air right away. Use the wave technique to begin your speech, and your sound will come out relaxed and rich. Use it in any other tight spots at the beginning of sentences. The beauty of the wave technique is that because you sound relaxed, you'll soon feel calmer mentally as well.

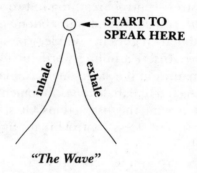

"The Wave"

3. *Quick relaxers.* You would warm up before running a 1,000-meter dash, wouldn't you? Here are three simple exercises to do just before an important talk. Duck into a restroom and whack the stress out of your system with the *Success Shake, the Stretch for Success,* and the *Confidence Collapse.*

The Success Shake: Stand up and for ten seconds shake out and wiggle all your extremities—legs, arms, hands, shoulders—and move your head around. If you feel silly, all the better, since that makes it harder for you to feel scared.

Stretch for Success: Pick a point on the ceiling and imagine the word *success* written there. Stretch your hands toward it ten times. Really reach and feel the stretch as you go for that goal.

Confidence Collapse: To be done only if you have a strong back! Bend over at the waist, letting your neck and arms hang loose. Then come up slowly, vertebra by vertebra. When your shoulders are erect, say with confidence, "I'm ready!" Do this again after your speech, if you like, and announce, "I did it!" as a way of recognizing your accomplishment.

> **You can control nervousness
> before it controls you.**

• I'm Afraid I'll Go Blank

Believe it or not, it is normal for your mind to turn to mashed potatoes, especially at the beginning of your talk. To prevent disasters you have to increase the accessibility of the relevant information in your brain. The following strategies will help you recall your material, even when your whole career seems to be riding on one talk.

Three Steps to Blank-out Prevention

1. *Overprepare.* Remember preparation, not desperation. Think of preparation as an insurance policy against going blank—and it also helps you recover if disaster does strike. If a speaking event is important to you, have your outline ready a week in advance. That week leaves plenty of time for the next blank-out prevention tip.

2. *Rehearse.* Note that the word *rehearse* contains the word *rehear.* Practicing out loud or in your head over a week's time allows your brain to gradually and reliably store key points for easy recall. It is far more effective to space out your practice, rehearsing twice a day for a week, than to try to ram it all into your head the night before. If you do not have the luxury of a week's notice, the third blank-out tip is especially critical.

3. *Useful notes.* I'll say it louder—USEFUL NOTES! Many of my clients make notes that might as well be written in Sanskrit. Useful notes are large, brief, organized with lots of white space to a page, and preferably printed or typed. Most important, notes are not a prop you haul along for the big event, they are your major memory-jogging tool. So have them ready for your practice sessions too. Plan to glance at them every once in a while during your talk so there won't be any telltale shuffling or panicky staring when you really need your notes.

• What If I Do Go Blank?

Obviously, you will be struck by a lightning bolt and no one will ever talk to you again.

Seriously, even experienced speakers have moments when they look at the audience with a frozen stare and wonder, Who are these people? What am I doing here? And what on earth am I supposed to be talking about? The trick is to *accept* these uncomfortable moments and launch into Blank-out Recovery. Follow these guidelines:

1. Accept the blank-out. Say to yourself, "I've forgotten and it's uncomfortable, but I can recover."

2. Pause and glance at your notes. It will seem like an eternity to you but not to the audience. When clients blank out in a practice session, I always ask them afterward how long they think their silence lasted. They usually estimate recovery took ten times longer than it actually did. The glance at your notes will take a maximum of ten seconds. Trust me!

3. If you have no notes, you should still pause while you figure out what you want your next topic to be. It is essential not to panic at this moment. Smile—they'll think you're just gathering your energy. Remember that you haven't *lost* your mind, you're just *reorganizing* it.

4. Whether or not you have notes, you can also calmly ask the audience, "Now where was I?" Audiences are usually on your side. They don't want to see someone be humiliated any more than you want to make a fool of yourself. Chances are someone will pipe up with the last thing you said, and you can pick up right where you left off.

Michelle, a history professor who used to write out all her lectures, was concerned about her stiff delivery. In learning to speak from notes, she achieved a more natural speaking style but also experienced a few brief blank-outs. But she had trained herself not to overreact. She told herself, It's only a moment, found her next point in her notes, and the students hardly noticed that anything had happened. Knowing what to do when what she had feared actually happened was a crucial part of her dramatic improvement.

• What If They See I'm Nervous?

It is important to realize that it's possible to be quite nervous and still do a knock-out job. The major signs of nervousness, such as your heart beating a mile a minute, aren't really visible to the audience. And remember that you always perceive changes in your physiology more intensely than others do. In workshops where people coach one another, 90 percent of the time participants will say, "I was dying of nervousness," and everyone else will say sincerely, "You didn't look nervous." Sometimes people even say they were stuttering or stumbling, but the video shows no evidence of it. However, speech hesitation, dramatic voice changes, and sudden or abrupt movements *will* reveal your nervousness to the audience. Does it matter?

The worst an audience will think is, "He's nervous"—which is not an indictment of your smarts, sophistication, or mental health. In fact, most audiences will overlook a lot: sweating, dropping notes, shaking like a leaf. Just two things they will not forgive: lack of preparation and signs that you don't care how you take up their time. Nervousness is actually a sign of caring about your performance, not of incompetence. As long as you act as if your nervousness is not the end of the world for you, the audience will not tense up or judge you for it.

Signs of nervousness can even endear you to the audience. I'll never forget the time I faced a roomful of cold, uninterested faces, people who had been forced to listen to me. Unintentionally, I hit my coffee cup, spilling hot liquid all over the place. Far from making them resent me more, it loosened up the audience.

Should you confess to the audience that you're nervous? Yes, if doing so will help you feel less nervous *and* you can deliver your confession in a confident way. Jim, a bookstore owner speaking at a large conference for the first time, used this creative approach: "Lately I've been picking books out of the psychology section, and I ran across an interesting psychological syndrome called 'Capgras's syndrome,' where a person believes he stays at home while his other self, a dummy, goes out to take care of his business. Well, I'm glad to be here today because the real Jim is scared to death of public speaking." The supportive laughter he received definitely made him feel better as he went on.

Perhaps the best solution to worry that the audience will be on to your willies is to expect uncomfortable moments and have a plan that helps you take them in stride. Here are some tips for troubleshooting nervousness:

1. Prethink what might go wrong and how you'd handle it. From my experience of spilling coffee and seeing the audience warm up, I developed an exercise called "creating catastrophe." For practice, I encourage clients to act out the very worst thing that can happen and see that they can live through it. Whether you go blank, drop your notes, walk into a wall, or your wig comes loose, just fix it as best you can and go on.

2. If your nervousness does show, keep going and maintain a "so what" attitude. The audience will only be as nervous about your shaky voice or trembling hands as you are.

3. Use success thoughts like these at the moments you feel nervous:

> It's OK to be nervous.
> I can be nervous and still do well.
> Even if they notice I'm nervous, nothing bad will happen.

• I Wasn't Nervous Beforehand, but When I Got Up There I Thought I Was Having a Heart Attack

The surprise your body pulled on you is not uncommon, though most of us start feeling nervous before we get to the podium. According to researchers, increases in heart rate, blood pressure, and adrenaline flow, and other manifestations of stress begin before we speak and peak during the first few minutes that we face our audience.

Struggling through those first minutes successfully usually leads to a plateau phase where we feel relieved and might even begin to enjoy speaking to a group. Curiously, for some of us, the vital signs elevate again after the presentation is over. It could be a surge of relief or a stress reaction induced by the thought, I really loused that up!

Though the physical manifestations of your fear of speaking are scary and never pleasant, it's possible to prevent and control the worst reactions.

Scaring Away Speaking Fear

1. Get to know your "signature" stress reaction, the way you physically respond to stress. In addition to changes in heartbeat, blood pressure, and adrenaline, you might experience sweating, coldness, stomach rumbling or belching, dizziness, changes in breathing, loss of appetite, or blushing. All these responses are normal. If you will be speaking in front of a group for the first time, expect *some* type of physical change, especially at the beginning. An anticipated response is easier to handle than one that comes as a surprise.

2. Take these precautions to minimize physical reactions at the beginning of a talk:

   a. Avoid caffeine and other stimulants. They can make

you feel stage fright even if you're not scheduled to give a speech.

b. Eat something but not too much. If your body is too hungry, it releases adrenaline, which will key you up more. Overeating before a speech, however, may make you sluggish.

c. Avoid dairy products. They can coat your mouth and throat, giving you a gooky feeling and an unpleasant voice.

d. Don't drink alcoholic beverages. Though some people feel calmer and less inhibited after a cocktail, drinking may also noticeably affect both your speech and your thinking.

e. Avoid tranquilizers. If you feel your symptoms are so severe that you need medication, consult a physician trained in treating performance anxiety. He or she will advise you on whether or not medication will help.

3. Overprepare the first minute of what you will say, even if the content is not that important. Beginning confidently will minimize your feeling of being threatened up there.

4. Tell yourself, Though I feel uncomfortable, I can still handle this. It will become a self-fulfilling prophecy.

5. For a week before an important talk, practice relaxed breathing and visualize a successful presentation. Troubleshoot any potential rough spots even if you're not anxious in advance.

Ben, a manager in a computer firm, told me that his reactions in front of an audience were inconsistent. Sometimes he would stand up and carry it off like an old pro; other times he would feel his body going out of control, and he'd lose all concentration. Though Ben liked to "shoot from the hip," he knew that success in public speaking couldn't be a hit-or-miss affair. He began visualizing both the best and the worst physical stress scenarios for upcoming presentations and told me something I've repeated to other clients: It is better to imagine the worst thing in advance than to have the worst thing catch you by surprise in real life.

• I Get Freaked Out When an Audience Stares Blankly at Me

I agree, audiences can look creepy—it's not all in your head. Don't take the glacier gazes personally, though, since members of the audience are just being an audience. They are operating under the principles of audience psychology, obeying certain unspoken rules about how to act and how not to act. Knowing these rules should help you remain composed.

A Primer on Audience Psychology

1. *Audiences are cool, not comforting.* In other words, don't expect pats on the back and scads of smiles when you walk in the door. Curiously, though most people are scared of speaking themselves, they express little sympathy for the poor presenter up there all alone. So if they seem cold at first, remember that they'd be looking at any other speaker in the same cool way. For the most part you will have to give warmth before you get it. When an audience is staring blankly at you, the last thing you want to do is stare blankly back.

2. *Audiences are responders, not initiators.* They wait for the speaker to set the tone for how they're supposed to act. They won't relax until you act relaxed. They won't ask questions until you provide the opportunity to ask questions. Audiences will even usually sit in a formal, rigid posture until you signal (perhaps by moving away from the podium or leaning forward) that it's okay to stretch out. The good news, then, is that you're in the position to set the standard for the audience behavior you want.

3. *Audiences don't want to be noticed.* Audiences consist of individuals who don't want to be singled out. While the speaker worries about poor performance, they have their own concerns. They may fear introducing themselves (especially standing up

and introducing themselves), asking you a stupid question, being called on, or being volunteered for something they don't know how to do. Take a look at the first row of seats at your next conference—it often stays empty. Heaven forbid they get too near the speaker! The audience's need not to be noticed takes precedence over your need for a little nurturing.

While we're at it, one idea I've had is to offer a seminar called "How to Be a Good Audience." Its highlights would include:

1. Do something for the speaker. Give him nonverbal signals that he's OK. Smiles and nods will do fine. Remember, it's lonely up there.

2. Avoid behaviors that increase the speaker's paranoia. Don't whisper, file your nails, sneak peeks at the newspaper, gaze out the window, or fall asleep. You may *feel* invisible, but you're not.

THE GOLDEN RULE FOR AUDIENCES

Treat the speaker as you would like to be treated if you were speaking.

• I Hate to Introduce Myself to a Group

Especially when the leader goes around the room and you have to wait your turn, right? Though it seems strange to fear saying your own name and occupation, many people do. Many of my clients feel upset and confused by stage-fright symptoms that grow more intense as their turn approaches. They worry they'll say something stupid or go blank. What's wrong? they wonder.

Why You Hate Introducing Yourself to a Group

This seemingly easy situation actually has all five ingredients that increase apprehension for most people.

1. *Formality.* The more you consider a situation structured and formal, the more likely you are to feel stressed. Chatting away for an hour to the stranger in the next seat will almost always seem easier than getting up and speaking coherently about yourself for half a minute.

2. *Anticipation.* The more time we have to anticipate a speaking event, the more time we have to worry about how we'll do.

3. *The escape factor.* Whenever you feel you can't escape, fear increases. If you feel there's a comfortable way out, fear decreases. If they're going around a room and you're in it, you know they'll get to you.

4. *Time pressure.* You have to talk now or never, which is always more difficult than chiming in when you feel like it.

5. *Conspicuousness.* When you feel everyone is looking at you, stress increases. Having to walk to the front of the room for the introduction is much worse than introducing yourself from your chair.

How to Live Through Introducing Yourself to a Group

1. As you now know, it's normal to feel nervous. So don't get down on yourself for being anxious—you're not the only one.

2. Plan a sequence for introducing yourself. Here is a good format.

Say your name slowly: "I'm Ralph Gomez."

Next, say the main thing you want them to know: "I'm here to help the team develop writing skills."

Conclude with a "looking forward" statement: "I'm looking forward to getting to know each of you personally."

By all means use a touch of lightness or humor if it's your style, for example: "I'm the phantom phone person you've all been talking to for the last month."

3. Use diaphragmatic breathing and the Pick-a-tic technique (see "Is There a Quick Way to Get Rid of Nervousness?" on page 85) to stay calm while waiting to speak.

4. Use "the wave" for beginning (see "If Only I Could Relax . . ." on page 90).

5. Err on the side of informality, not formality. Smile and use a relaxed posture—perhaps one or both hands on your chair if you're standing. Introductions should convey approachability, not rigidity.

6. Make eye contact with two or more people during each phrase of your introduction.

7. End confidently. Either say nothing or "thank you" and turn your attention to the next victim. Avoid wimping out, as in these exits:

> "Well, I guess that's it."
> "Um, that's all."

....

My Presentation Is Next Week— Help!

• I Do a Lot Better One-on-One

Many of us freeze when our audience is larger than one. Face to face with one soul, it's easier to feel comfort and control for several reasons:

1. *Naturalness.* One-to-one communication is more conducive to a natural flow between speaker and listener roles. In presenting, especially in a formal setting, you usually hold the floor longer than you're used to.

2. *Closeness.* Ever notice that when you want to confide personal thoughts, feelings, or opinions to someone you instinctively lean forward? Physical closeness encourages intimacy. At a distance from many faces, numerous speakers stiffen up, revealing less emotion and fewer aspects of their personalities. The irony is that the best group speakers talk to an audience no differently from the way they'd talk to a guy across a table.

3. *Responsiveness.* Though we never totally know what a listener is thinking or feeling, the more listeners there are, the greater the number of unknowns. Also, people who are part of a group generally offer less nonverbal and verbal feedback. Consequently, the questions What are they thinking? and Am I making sense? become more troublesome.

Harry was remarkable for his quick climb in the banking industry and his flexible managerial skills. But in order to be promoted to executive level in his bank, he needed to get comfortable speaking to the bank officers and trustees as a group. Harry communicated easily with all the officers as individuals—they were big fans of his, in fact. We worked on isolating the communication behaviors that worked for him one on one and incorporating them into the way he spoke at his next board meeting. Here is the list he came up with, to help those of you with Harry's problem develop more naturalness, closeness, and audience responsiveness with groups.

Harry's Tips for Unfreezing Before Groups

1. To increase naturalness, continue to:
   - sound conversational (don't become overly formal).
   - use gestures (don't turn into a robot).
   - make unplanned comments (not all remarks have to be scripted).
   - be willing to be less than perfect (one-to-one or in a group, you needn't be faultless to do fine).

2. To increase closeness:
   - move away from the podium if the room's acoustics permit it.
   - with a small group, sit with them at the table.
   - establish emotional closeness by looking relaxed and animated (don't lose your personality).

3. To increase responsiveness:
   - *ask* for feedback. ("Does this make sense?" "Anyone have any thoughts to add to that?")
   - increase participation with the suggestions in "How Do I Get Audience Participation?" (see page 136).

• I Don't Know How to Organize a Talk

Begin organizing your thoughts by distinguishing between what the audience needs to know and what you'd like to tell. Find out as much as possible about the audience so that you can include information that connects with their concerns, expectations, and level of sophistication. For example, though I speak about communication in general all the time, a nurse wants to know how to communicate when wearing a surgical mask, while a hairdresser wants to know how to establish eye contact through a mirror. Decide what you most want the audience to know as a result of listening to you—three new ways to find clients, the latest research on superconductors—and weed out irrelevant information.

Next, decide how long you want to talk and have audience members talk, as well as the style of speaking that seems appropriate. Will you strike a logical tone with research, facts, statistics, and graphs, or use a more emotional approach with humor, opinions, anecdotes, interpretations, and self-disclosure? Think about the character of the audience and the occasion, and your own strengths.

Then use *The Four Ws* to plan a structure for your talk.

1. **W**here are we headed? When you begin to speak, listeners will be wondering what's going to be happening. They need some orientation and structure from the speaker. By summarizing your agenda and mentioning various housekeeping details (about length, breaks, handouts, and so forth), listeners will feel more secure and you'll feel more grounded and focused.

2. **W**hy should we care? This step requires some creativity and persuasiveness. Polite as they may look, audiences are always thinking, "What's in it for me?" Your goal is to let them know, directly or indirectly, how listening to you will benefit

them. Conventionally, you accomplish this by appealing to the audience's needs or fears.

> "As you know, the company has been in a slump since the takeover. All of us are concerned about our job security and investment in the company, so we have a lot to do in the next hour to come up with creative marketing ideas."

Some speakers do well with a more unusual hook. Regina, a nurse, was struggling with a talk she had to give to community groups about the importance of eye care. She told me that four of her recent talks had flopped. When I asked what would spark people's interest, she said, "They're afraid of someday not being able to see." And suddenly she had an inspiration. She opened her next talk by asking the audience to close their eyes, saying, "Imagine what it would be like if your world was like this all the time." It worked, she later told me—all eyes stayed open for the rest of her presentation.

Similarly, Mark, who conducted seminars on quitting smoking, felt frustrated because too many smokers would leave his introductory sessions without signing up for the course. He devised a new strategy involving a series of questions that would make listeners feel bad about smoking and good about quitting, along these lines:

> "How many of you would make at least one important person in your life happy if you quit smoking? How many of you would like to be around to watch your grandchildren grow up? Have you ever been told you smell like smoke? . . . If you answered yes to any of these questions, this is where you belong tonight."

Not only did more people sign up, people were more friendly to him because he had made personal contact.

You can, if you wish, switch the order of steps one and two. Both styles offer effective openings.

3. What's it all about? This section comprises the bulk of your speech and requires the most planning. First generate a

random list of all the points, examples, and experiences you might include in your talk. Next screen them, using this checklist:

_____Will the audience benefit from hearing this?
_____Can this be left out without any harm?
_____Am I including this for me or for them?
_____Is this too detailed for this occasion?
_____Will including this take away from my main points?

Then take some time to generate an order for the points you want to include. It may help to write each point on an index card and shuffle them around until an order clicks. Be sure to include a balance between facts and information on the one hand, and examples, experiences, and anecdotes on the other. Finally, summarize the order you choose in a detailed diagram or visually clear, step-by-step outline with major headings, subtopics, and examples indicated.

4. **Well . . . ?** At the end of your talk you need to pull things together in some way so that your most important points reverberate in the listeners' minds, and they know what, if anything, they need to do to apply your message. Some concluding strategies to consider:

Extracting a major theme: "So from all these examples we can see that we really have a long way to go in meeting the letter of the law in child custody matters."

Appeal to emotions: "Remember Timmy, whose hardworking parents became sick without medical insurance? He is still homeless. Timmy and thousands of other homeless kids in this city need your help."

Practical action to take: "Here's a petition to urge our congressman to defeat that bill. I hope you'll sign."

Coming attractions: "So that's what you need to know to draw up your own will. Next week I'll get into do-it-yourself divorces."

• Should I Use Notes, Memorize My Talk, or What?

Ideally, you will use notes, which I define as word cues that help you remember whole thoughts. Notes allow you to be more conversational and let you put your main focus on the audience, where it belongs. However, if it's your first talk or a very important or formal presentation, such as at an academic conference, it might be better to speak from a prepared text. If you decide to write out your speech, see "How Can I Make Good Eye Contact If I Need to Use a Script?" (page 116) because there is a crucial difference between using a script and sounding scripted.

On the other hand, if you are the kind of person who has a hard time composing fluid sentences or if cleverness, preciseness, or entertainment is crucial to the speech, consider memorizing at least parts of your remarks. Memorizing helps you concentrate more on delivery because you won't have to worry about which words to use. Make sure you have notes even if you memorize, though—a lesson Winston Churchill learned the hard way. Churchill, who became one of history's greatest orators, blanked out during one of his early speeches in Parliament. After trailing off in the middle of a sentence, he fumbled in his pockets, then sat down and covered his face with his hands. Though he never again blanked out, for the rest of his career he took out insurance before every speech by preparing detailed notes.

Some of my clients resist the idea of using notes. "No one in my company does," they say. Or "I'll look overprepared." If you have this concern, put your notes together with other papers connected with the business at hand and refer to them only when you need reminders of what you had planned to say.

Using notes, you will still need to familiarize yourself with your talk. That means practice—as much practice as time allows. Follow these practice guidelines, and by the time you face the audience, your talk will be as familiar to you and as easy to get across as your name, address, and social security number.

How to Practice Using Notes

1. Begin your practice sessions as soon as you've finished organizing your material. (See "I Don't Know How to Organize a Talk" on page 109 for advice on putting your thoughts into order.) Find a time and place where you won't be interrupted, review your notes, and practice out loud as if the audience were in the room with you.

2. Look down, scan your first cue, let that evoke a complete idea, and speak. When you finish that thought, look down, scan the next cue, let that evoke the next idea, and speak. For example, in one seminar leader's notes, two words, *lead time*, prompt her to speak for several minutes about the fact that it typically takes a year or more for an author to write a book and nine to twelve additional months for a publisher to turn a finished manuscript into a published book.

3. If an item in your notes doesn't smoothly evoke a thought, you need either a different cue or more detailed notes. Rethink your idea, talk yourself through it, and adjust your notes. A fuller version of the "lead time" idea, for example, might be as follows:

> Lead time—time it takes to turn idea into finished book
> 1 yr (optimistic) to write
> 9–12 mos to produce
> So: What's hot now might not be in 2 yrs
> Ex: aerobics, Dan Quayle

After practice and some tinkering with your notes, you'll be able to scan your notes and begin the next item in only two or three seconds. Except for a few parts you may want to memorize—the first thing you plan to say, the last thing, and any stories or jokes you're hoping will elicit laughs—you'll be delivering the same thoughts, though your words will be somewhat different each time you run through the speech.

4. If possible, practice before D-Day with a friend, relative, or colleague for an audience. Ask specific questions afterward to get genuinely useful feedback: Were there any confusing points? Any sections that seemed rough? Any parts that dragged or seemed rushed?

Add reminders to your notes indicating where you need to pause, slow down, or emphasize a particular point.

• Where Should I Look When I'm Speaking to an Audience?

If you view the audience as piranhas, you'll grab any chance to avoid looking them in the eye. Lisa, a friendly, charming woman who had just been elected president of a large national church group, was dreading her first talk to the state leaders in her organization. She asked me if it was OK to aim her speech at the clock in the back of the church she'd be speaking in. "Surely," I suggested, "you can find a face in the audience more friendly than the one on the clock."

In order to see people in your audience for what they are—people—master the eye-contact techniques I taught Lisa. Your listeners will see you as warmer and more influential.

1. *Warm up.* Get the good feeling of relating well to your audience by making small talk with several individuals before your talk begins. Then when all eyes are on you, you won't be confronting a mass of strangers.

2. *Follow the "Rule of Three."* If you're new at public speaking, pick three specific people to focus on—one in the middle, one on the right, and one on the left of the room. These audience members will be your eye-contact landmarks as you scan the room. Be careful, though, not to look at any one person for more than about five seconds. It's creepy being stared at by the speaker!

3. *Do the one-minute scan.* Include everyone in your audience by scanning the people in the room about once a minute while you're talking. You will have a tendency to focus more attention on the folks directly in front of you. That's all right, but be sure you don't ignore those to your right and left.

4. *Learn the art of "nose contact."* If you are speaking to a small audience (three to thirty people), it's not necessary to look right into their eyes. Just glance at the center of a listener's face (usually his nose). It'll suffice.

• How Can I Make Good Eye Contact If I Need to Use a Script?

When you must read a text to a group, making good eye contact with your audience—as well as with your notes—gets tricky. When reading something aloud, your natural tendency is to keep your head down. TV personalities are lucky: A teleprompter that scrolls their words on a small screen allows them to keep their heads up while reading. That's why their presentation seems so smooth. They rarely need to look down because the words are right up there in front of them.

With just a typewriter or a computer printer, however, you can devise a homemade equivalent to a teleprompter. First, type or print out your speech with three to seven words per line. It will look like poetry, not prose, on the page, with the line breaks at places where you would naturally insert a slight or a significant pause while reading. For example, you might arrange the previous paragraph like this:

When you must read a text
to a group,
making good eye contact
with your audience
—as well as with your notes—
gets tricky.
When reading something aloud,
your natural tendency
is to keep your head down.

TV personalities
are lucky:

A teleprompter

on a small screen
allows them to keep their heads up
while reading.
That's why their presentation seems so smooth.
They rarely need to look down
because the words
are right up there
in front of them.

Because each line contains only as many words as you can take in at a glance, you'll be able to look at the audience more often, with less chance of losing your place. Looking down to take in the next line or group of lines and looking up again at the audience takes only a second. Remember that whenever you're talking, your head should be *up*, not down. This formula should help:

LOOK DOWN, SCAN, REMEMBER, AND LOOK UP

Here are some other tips for preparing a script for effective delivery:

1. Use only the top ¾ of each page so that your eyes won't need to go too far down.

2. Add accent marks or underlining to words and phrases you want to emphasize.

3. Break words that are hard to pronounce into syllables or spell them as they are pronounced.

4. Make sure the words and the sentence structures you choose are conversational, not bookish. When you practice, revise any sentence that trips you up.

5. End each page of notes with a complete sentence to avoid having to turn a page mid-sentence.

Arranging your text for effective delivery also helps you become familiar with it after fewer rehearsals without sounding scripted. Practice a few times, and your audience will think you're speaking fluently from notes, not reading!

• What Should I Do With My Hands?

Many clients mistakenly believe that hands should be hidden from view. Consequently, they dream up all kinds of ingenious hand tricks: hands secreted under the podium, hands clasped Indian-style behind their back, and hands military-style at their sides. Short of chopping them off, folks go to amazing lengths not to "talk with their hands."

Forget it. The best thing hands can do is to convey naturally, without much orchestration, the conviction and enthusiasm of your message. To discover exactly what your hands should be doing in front of an audience, take a look at how you use them when you think no one is watching—in one-to-one conversation, at dinner, or on the telephone. Then keep these tips in mind to make your gestures influential and relaxed as you "reach out" to a group.

Thumbs down for:
- Moving arms wildly about.
- Making a hand gesture with no purpose.
- Repeating the same gesture over and over.
- Fiddling with or wringing hands.
- Keeping hands in any one tense position (like in your pockets) for too long.
- Folding hands over your crotch (known to speech coaches as the "figleaf position") or in other embarrassing positions. And for gosh sakes, keep hands away from your nose or mouth!
- Keeping hands very close to your body—looks wimpy.
- Letting fingers hang loose—looks really wimpy.

Thumbs up for:
- Observing and using gestures that come naturally.
- Keeping gestures above the waist and directing them outward for visibility and influence.

- Punctuating key thoughts and words with gestures.
- Using a variety of influential arm and hand positions, including one or two hands outstretched, palms facing upward, or parallel to each other.
- Using finger enumeration to designate points one, two, three.
- Resting one hand lightly on the desk or lectern while you use the other hand to gesture.

Don't just stand there—GESTICULATE!

• Do I Need to Tell Jokes in a Presentation?

Yes, go ahead and tell a joke if *all* of the following apply:

- Your joke makes sense for the topic and the environment.
- You can immediately tie in the joke with the larger theme for the presentation.
- Your joke is simple and short—audiences can't remember more than three types of guys meeting Saint Peter at Heaven's gate.
- Your joke won't offend women, Caucasians, blacks; Protestants, Catholics, Jews, Seventh-Day Adventists; Republicans, Democrats, independents; cat, dog, fish, or bird lovers; people who don't like jokes; and so forth.
- You like telling jokes and not just for speeches.
- Not only that, you're *good* at telling jokes, especially for speeches.

Otherwise, don't tell a joke.

If you flunked the above checklist, remember that there are other forms of humor besides jokes. Here are some suggestions for being jocular without telling a joke:

1. *Use exaggeration.* One presenter who had the misfortune of following an extraordinary speaker at a conference began by saying, "That was a superb talk, Carl. I'm reminded of the time I tried out for the opera, and the fellow before me was either Pavarotti or his twin."

2. *Use real-life examples with a silly slant or a bizarre bent.* A woman in my speaking-under-stress class shared this with the group: "I always thought my talks went pretty well, but my boss disagrees. He says I begin well and end well. But in the middle,

he says, I always faint, and he's getting a little tired of reviving me."

3. *Use a touch of self-deprecation.* Audiences respond well to a speaker who is able to laugh at herself. Be careful, however, that you put yourself down only when you have the group's confidence. Otherwise, they may perceive you as a loser, not as humorously humble. A professor who received utter silence when he asked his graduate class a question did get a laugh when he said, "Now I know my questions are extremely thought-provoking, but don't all jump to answer at once."

• I Feel So Awkward After I'm Introduced

It's natural to feel uncomfortable between the time the spotlight falls on you and the moment when you begin to fill up the room's silence with your speech. Use these *Ready-Go-Ready* reminders to help you feel in control, make a confident impression from the very beginning, and avoid embarrassing surprises such as tripping on the way to the platform.

Ready

1. Prevent mistakes in your introduction that might fluster you by speaking to the introducer beforehand, explaining how to pronounce your name if that can be a problem and checking to make sure he will correctly identify you. One way to control how you will be introduced is to type out the points about yourself that you'd like emphasized on an index card, and say, "You might want to use this in your introduction . . ."

2. Preplan what you'll take with you up to the platform. Don't lug along so much that you look like a bag person. If you're a woman, avoid carrying your purse; find a safe place beforehand to stash it.

3. Make sure your notes are packaged in a way that looks good. Cameron, a vice president of an insurance company, showed me a videotape of a speech he had spent a lot of time preparing for. Despite his elegant designer suit and well-planned spiel, he got off to a bad start when he pulled a crumpled sheet of paper out of his pocket. It looked sloppy. A dark folder or thin three-ring binder looks classier and works well. Make sure your pages or cards are clearly marked and numbered. Don't staple your notes so you need to flip pages. If you use a paper clip, remove it before you begin.

4. After you're introduced, you don't want to have to struggle out of a seat in the middle of a long row with an elephant-

sized person blocking the end. Before it's your turn, change seats or find an unobtrusive place to stand so you'll have a clearer, shorter path to the front of the room. Notice whether there are any stairs, wires, plugs, or anything else that could cause a stumble along the way.

5. Become aware of any automatic grooming movements you make when you're getting ready to go onstage, such as hitching up your pants, straightening your tie, or adjusting your hair, and do whatever it is *before* you're introduced. Keep your shoes and jacket on—you don't really want to get dressed in front of all those people, do you? Remember that as soon as you're introduced, eyes will be on you even before you reach the platform.

Go

Walk up to the podium in a slow and confident manner. Wear a warm facial expression so you'll look human even if no one is smiling at you. Be aware of the stairs, cords, or other obstacles you've previously checked out.

Ready

Once you arrive at the podium, take a moment to prepare your environment there. Place your notes where you'll need them, pour a glass of water for yourself, and check the height of the microphone if necessary. It's all right for there to be a brief pause. Then look up, smile, and pick out one person to start talking to. This quiet time can feel like half a year to the speaker, but as long as you don't fumble or apologize, the audience's first impression of you will be a strong one.

• How Do I Warm Up the Audience?

Mostly by being genuine. You'll melt the ice and warm up the room by helping the audience view you as a total human being rather than a rhetorical robot. Even better, establishing contact with the audience takes away the stress of being in an abnormal situation and allows you to feel like "you" rather than a distant relative of your regular self. In addition to the suggestions in "If Only I Could Relax . . ." (page 90), there are numerous tricks that experienced presenters use to unfreeze the atmosphere. Try the ones that feel comfortable to you, and never forget the impact of a well-meant smile.

Twenty-one Ways to Warm Up an Audience:

1. Arrive early. Make small talk and learn at least a few names before you begin.

2. If possible, make sure people have name tags that are large enough for you to read. This requires advance planning because usually names are written too small or too faintly.

3. Ask audience members to introduce themselves to one other person and find out something specific about their partner. ("Let your partner know one communication strength you have and one communication skill you'd like to develop.")

4. Have the audience complete a brief survey beforehand and include the results in your talk. ("This method is especially good for the 59 percent who said in the survey that diets just don't work for you.")

5. Before you begin, invite volunteers to let you know what they most want to know about your subject. ("What are your most burning questions about the new tax legislation?")

6. Bring in humorous items and newspaper clippings espe-

cially relevant to this audience. Start collecting them well in advance of your talk.

7. Make references to tidbits about their world. ("I understand you've been preoccupied with moving your offices this month.")

8. Conduct a poll as part of your talk. ("How many of you have ever been scuba diving?")

9. Ask rhetorical questions (where you are not expecting a real answer out loud from anyone). Pause. Your audience will be answering in their own minds before you go on.

10. Use cartoons on handouts or slides.

11. Refer to information about the audience that you have gathered before the presentation or from the introductions. ("If you're a lawyer, like Mike, or a tennis pro, like Patsy . . .")

12. Situate yourself physically closer to the audience— move away from the podium.

13. Bring candies, fruit, or mints for a thoughtful touch.

14. Provide enough breaks!

15. Deviate from your main outline to give some spontaneous-sounding asides.

16. Use fill-in-the-blank handouts so that people complete them as you go through your talk. Your audience will stay mentally alert anticipating what might come next. For instance:

TWENTY-ONE WAYS TO WARM UP AN AUDIENCE
  1.
  2.
  3.

17. Do something surprising. Bring in an unusual or clever object. (One client showed a giant sponge to demonstrate the resilience of the marketplace.)

18. Ask for a volunteer to help with keeping notes or demonstrating your product. If it's a close-knit audience, when you connect with one, you'll connect with all.

19. Build in opportunities to show a range of emotions— you'll look more human.

20. Bring up their objections before they do. It will show your broadmindedness. ("I know many of you find it difficult to think about life insurance at this stage of the game.")

21. Reveal relevant personal experiences. People will identify with you more easily.

• Should I Use Visual Aids?

The odds that your audience will receive and absorb your message improve when you include a visual component in your presentation. Anything your audience can see, from a wave of your hand to a ten-screen slide show, adds additional impact. Communication researchers have found that while audiences remember less than 10 percent of what they hear, they retain about 50 percent of what they hear *and* see.

Audience desire to see something entertaining has increased greatly as people spend more time watching TV. Rock bands, for example, have found that it's not enough just to play the music. On their 1989 world tour, the Rolling Stones gave their fans the satisfaction of lasers, lights, films, and a forty-foot honky-tonk woman, along with great rock 'n' roll.

The emphasis on big productions has had its drawbacks for those of us who have been content to stand up and say a few words. Many clients worry about going onstage without fancy visuals. The opposite problem can occur as well. If your company is willing to spend big bucks for a smooth and flashy slide show, many speakers would just as soon fade into the background.

Dr. Levine, an excellent speaker who promoted health care plans to corporations, came to see me because he felt packaged presentations cramped his style. No wonder. Charts, graphs, and time lines were inhibiting his sharp wit and story-telling talent. He had also developed the habit of switching on a slide and studying it before speaking, as if the slide were telling him what to do. Dr. Levine and I agreed that it was foolish to lose potential business because someone had put together a slide show he felt obligated to use.

We developed Levine's Laws, principles to guide you no matter what types of visuals you are using:

1. Outstanding visuals can never in themselves be more powerful than an outstanding presenter.
2. Make sure you control what the visuals say; don't let them control what you say.

And now for some finer points . . .

Showing Your Best With Visuals

1. Use professionally prepared slides when you want an image of polish and formality. Transparencies for overhead projectors require more handling and attention but create less distance between you and the group.

2. Make sure that any words on slides, transparencies, or flip charts are large and distinct enough for everyone in the audience to see. People get really peeved if they can't read your visuals.

3. Do not assume any equipment will work right. Always test projectors and so forth beforehand, and have extra bulbs on hand.

4. Don't overapologize if the slide projector breaks or the slides are upside-down. Say what should be:

"This should be right side up."
"This should be working once we get an extension cord."

If the problem can't be solved, make a decision to move ahead or do without.

5. Introduce each visual before showing it. You build a bit of anticipation this way, and it helps you guide the picture rather than vice versa. Of course, this requires either good notes or a good memory.

6. Consider the talk-and-write technique to add dynamism. Write or illustrate key concepts as you go along—this looks quick-witted and spontaneous. A clever client lightly penciled in key words on easel paper in advance. During the presentation they reminded her what to talk about or write next.

7. Don't expect your visuals to do the talking for you. They should reinforce key aspects of your message, not read like pages from a book. Use:

- bulleted words
- short phrases
- like this

8. Use the key words on your visuals as springboards, embellishing them by speaking about related facts and examples.

9. Don't show too much information at once. Your audience will just read ahead. Keep what you are talking about and what they are looking at in harmony.

10. Decide how you will situate yourself relative to the screen and the audience. If you randomly look at the visuals, then your notes, then the audience, you'll appear to lack focus. Use a pointer to interact with your material if possible. If you want to have presence, be present, not hidden in the back corner in the dark reading from a script.

11. Orient your audience by telling them where you want them to focus, particularly on a chart or graph.

"This chart shows the increase in smiling among Americans since 1950. Let's look at the dip in 1965 and explore . . ."

12. Remember to use yourself as your most versatile visual aid. Energetic speakers offer a host of visually interesting behaviors. Move around, change your posture, get away from the lectern, gesture, point, demonstrate, draw, remove your jacket (you'll look like you're getting down to business), walk a few steps and stop, take off your glasses, and so on.

• Microphones Intimidate Me

Since the microphone merely allows your message to be heard, it should weigh on your mind no more than your ballpoint pen does when you write. Yet many clients view the mike as a monster rather than an ally for audibility. Ava, a tax attorney who successfully taught tax law to small groups of associates in her firm, was asked to convey the same information at a state conference for recent law school graduates. As the conference approached, she confessed she was a nervous wreck. Why? Every mistake would be amplified, she wouldn't know how to talk into "the thing," and she'd sound so loud she wouldn't be able to think. By correcting these misconceptions about microphones and explaining how to handle different types of equipment, I helped Ava put her attention where it belonged: on conveying complicated tax laws to her audience.

Reminders for Microphone Mastery

1. The microphone's job is to amplify your normal voice. It works for you—you don't have to work for it. There is no need to strain or shout with a mike. Speak at your usual conversational volume. Since some microphones are sensitive to *p, b,* and *s* sounds, you may want to say these sounds a bit more quietly or with less air pressure.

2. A microphone picks up all sounds, not just speech. Beware of clinking jewelry, pens, or glasses, and of anything hitting the mike. Since rustling paper will sound like a crackling bonfire, put your notes on stiff cards or paper that won't make much noise.

3. A microphone can't distinguish between talk that you want your audience to hear and private comments you whisper within range of it. If there is a mike, assume it's on. Don't turn

to your fellow panelist and tell him that the audience looks dead!

4. Try to find out in advance what kind of mike you'll be using. Here are the different types and the pros and cons of each.

Lavaliere: hangs on a cord around your neck, leaving your hands free. It also frees you to move around, but you might need an extension cord to give you maximum range of movement. Stay conscious of the cord so you don't trip on it if you walk around.

Clip-on: same principle as the lavaliere; usually clipped on to the lapel of a jacket. Women should keep this in mind when planning what to wear and choose a dress or a jacket with a collar.

Hand-held: has to become part of your act because you control its position. You need to be careful not to keep adjusting the distance between your mouth and the mike, or your volume will be annoyingly inconsistent. This one is best if you're a crooner or someone who feels more secure with something to hold.

Stationary: doesn't budge; fixed to the lectern and adjustable in height. Since it will not relay your voice unless your breath stream is directed toward it, this mike restricts your range of movement but not your hand gestures. Usually you can turn your head right or left but not move a foot away.

Stand-up: picture the early radio show comedy teams. This restricts your movement and also leaves you more exposed because you're without a lectern. Most often the mike can be unfastened from the stand and held by hand.

5. The ideal mouth-to-mike distance varies, so experiment. The distance from your elbow to your fingertips is a good average distance for a stationary mike, and a fist's length usually works for a hand-held one. Never pucker your lips right up against the mike—that's much too close.

6. Try to arrive early for a mike check and a chance to get accustomed to the sound change (if any) in your amplified voice.

• What's the Best Room Arrangement for a Presentation?

How the tables and chairs are arranged forms an important part of the visual image and atmosphere you create in public speaking. The room arrangement affects how you relate to your group: Are you in a semicircle to show equal status, or are you looking down forebodingly at the audience from behind a lectern on a raised podium? Your chosen setup affects how group members interact with one another as well.

The arrangement ought to suit both the group and the goal of the session. I remember the time a client ushered me into a room set up for an interpersonal skills workshop designed to teach employees how to handle conflict better. The moment I stepped into the room I knew World War III might begin by lunchtime. My host had set twenty chairs in a circle for people who didn't like one another much to begin with and were now, because of the setup, feeling pressured to communicate. I suggested people rearrange the chairs in a less face-to-face fashion, and the tension lessened.

Tips for Making Arrangements

1. Decide what kind of atmosphere you want to foster:

   - formal versus informal
   - peer relationship to audience versus authoritative relationship to audience
   - maximum group interaction versus minimum group interaction
   - emphasis on information versus emphasis on feelings

2. To the extent that a room offers flexibility (there may be a table too large to move or chairs with desk arms and no tables),

choose the arrangement that best suits the atmosphere you want to create.

3. If you have carte blanche beforehand to specify the kind of room you want and how it's equipped as well as how it's arranged, here are some additional factors to consider:

- The size of the room in relation to the expected size of the group. Too big a room can be depressing; a small room can feel confining.
- The kind of table surface available (tables and chairs are much more comfortable for taking notes than the chair-with-arm type of desk).
- Whether you need a table or a lectern for notes, props, or your own comfort (this will rule some of the above options in or out).

You may or may not be able to specify your preferred arrangement, but always arrive early so you can check that everything is in the best shape possible.

ROOM ARRANGEMENTS

a) Circle

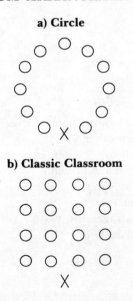

b) Classic Classroom

c) Squared-off "U"

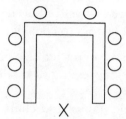

d) Semicircle

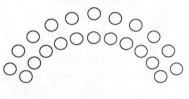

e) Square

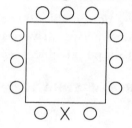

Type	*Advantages*	*Disadvantages*
a) Circle	Allows participants to see each other	Creates a touchy-feely tone if no tables
	Conducive to expressing ideas and opinions	Unwieldy with a very large group
	Leader can join circle as an equal	Uncomfortable for some people if leader needs to use blackboard, slides, or flip chart
	Encourages shy people to participate	Participants sitting next to the leader may feel uncomfortable

ROOM ARRANGEMENTS *(continued)*

Type	*Advantages*	*Disadvantages*
b) Classic Classroom (participants in rows, with you in front)	Conducive to imparting information Convenient for use of visual aids Enhances focus on leader's authority People feel comfortable taking notes	Adults strongly associate setup with school Feels artificial with a small group Discourages spontaneity and interaction People in the back may feel invisible or left out
c) Squared-off "U" (tables like three sides of a square, with you in front)	Allows interaction Squareness sets a more businesslike tone than the circle or semicircle Lots of room for you to move around in the middle of the "U" Convenient for use of visual aids	Space in the middle can make the whole room feel empty Won't work well with more than about twenty people
d) Semicircle (with you in front)	Multiple rows can accommodate more people than circle or squared-off "U" Lets leader be both authoritative and open to group participation	Can feel more crowded than circle or classic classroom
e) Square (one large table or small ones forming a large one)	Better than circle for taking notes Fosters more team spirit than the other options	Possibly not enough elbow room, particularly for left-handers Can get cluttered with distracting items

• How Do I Get Audience Participation?

A Chinese proverb says, "Tell me something, I'll forget; show me, I'll remember; involve me, I'll understand." According to recent studies, when people participate in a presentation, the material becomes at least three times more memorable for them than if they merely listened to a lecture. Sometimes you risk losing an audience altogether if you don't go out of your way to involve members.

Tani, a yoga instructor, once faced an after-dinner audience that would have fazed most speakers. It was an all-male group, many of whom had had a lot to drink, and when she was introduced, they laughed and catcalled as if she were a stripper. She immediately realized that the conventional lecture on stress-reduction techniques she had planned would be a disaster. Instead she stepped up to the microphone and announced, "I'm going to show you how to be more successful than you ever dreamed you could be. Close your eyes . . ." The men were so startled that most complied, and soon virtually everyone was quiet as Tani led them through a guided visualization that made them deeply relaxed.

Chances are you will never face a group as hostile as Tani's, but you can pull the average, distant audience over to your side by planning to use one of the following participation promoters.

1. Have audience members complete a quiz prior to your talk so they'll feel involved with your subject even before you begin talking. For example, a university health and safety officer quizzed people on what they presently knew about fire safety and corrected common myths and misconceptions during his talk.

2. Try a buzz session. Give partners or small groups a problem to solve within a designated short period of time. When time is up, say, "Buzz!" Example: "Come up with three ways to

improve our staff meetings." Have one member from each group announce its results to everyone else.

3. Using the case-study method, hand out a detailed problem or situation and give audience members some time to think before asking them how they would recommend attacking the problem. This may work well with subgroups too.

4. Brainstorm together. Ask the group a question and record all responses on a blackboard or easel. Explain that the goal is to come up with as many ideas as possible, regardless of practicality. Examples: What factors will affect the travel industry in the next decade? What are some ways we can enhance our community relations?

5. Use games, demonstrations involving audience members, and unusual objects to get a point across. John Albach, founder of the National Stuttering Project, teaches workshop participants how to juggle balls as a way for them to learn how to achieve balance and establish priorities in life.

6. Ask questions that invite input from volunteers, such as, "What methods of soliciting business do you already know about?" Recording the answers on a blackboard or flip chart will make others more inclined to contribute.

7. Throughout your talk, stop every once in a while and ask for comments or questions. Make sure you pause long enough to let someone chime in. Invite disagreement too.

• What If They Ask a Question I Can't Answer?

Some speakers cope with their fear of facing questions they can't answer by running way past the time when they're supposed to open the floor for questions. There are, however, credible ways to handle questions that stump you. Far from confirming you as an incompetent ignoramus, the following strategies will reinforce your professionalism.

Fielding Questions Like an Expert

When an audience member asks a question that you can't answer, *don't:*

- bluff or make up an answer
- offer an irrelevant answer
- put down the questioner
- simply say "I don't know" and go on to the next question

As a speaker you have a responsibility to be as helpful as possible to your listeners. You should point the way to an answer, and precisely how you can do that will depend on the situation. Some possibilities:

1. During an instructional course or tour that has several sessions:

"You know, that's a really good question and I'm going to get into that tomorrow." (Then find out the answer overnight.)

2. With an audience that has professional experience that may be different from yours:

"Any of you nutritionists want to offer an answer to that one?"

Even better, if you know people in the audience who are better qualified than you to answer, send the question on to them in a deferential way:

> "Caroline, do you want to answer that one?"

3. Where one listener asks for specific advice or information you don't have at your fingertips, offer to get him an answer later:

> "As people become more and more health conscious, cholesterol content is certainly a big concern to many noodle eaters. If you will give me your card afterward, I'd be glad to send you the latest information."

4. When the question is clever and catches you off guard, take the focus off how lamebrained you feel and acknowledge the questioner's insight and intelligence:

> "The role of the nose in human communication—now that's an issue I've never thought about. Perhaps anthropologists like Desmond Morris or Ray Birdwhistle have written something about that."

5. When you should know the answer as an expert and you're on the spot, find an angle to the question that you *can* answer:

> "Though I'm not aware of any research on the role of the nose in human communication, there has been quite a bit written on the role of facial expressions. For example . . ."

• I Don't Know How to Handle Idiotic, Repetitive, or Hostile Questions

Audiences say the darndest things sometimes. Someone asks virtually the same question you answered two minutes ago. At a prestigious scientific meeting, someone raises his hand and asks you how big a millimeter is. After a presentation on how to choose a therapist, a woman divulges her marital problems and asks how her marriage can be saved. Or you have just read what you thought was a touching story about a grandmother and someone stands to denounce you vehemently for perpetuating stereotypes of older people. Or despite the dozens of provocative ideas you have offered, all arms stay down when the moderator asks for questions.

The spontaneity that is part of the purpose of a question-and-answer period often brings surprises. While you can't predict the zingers, you can use certain strategies to remain competent, credible, personable, and poised. (See "What If They Ask a Question I Can't Answer?" on page 138 for some additional tips.)

Minding Your Ps and Qs During Q & A

1. Always repeat the question unless a moderator does so for you. Not only does this ensure that everyone in the room heard the question, it gives you a few extra moments to think up an appropriate response.

2. If your reputation or your company's reputation is on the line at your talk, try to anticipate the touchiest questions and come prepared with data to back your position up.

3. When a hostile question hits, control your urge to reach out and strangle the questioner. Your image will be enhanced if

you respond in a calm and confident manner. Control the length of your answer since hostile questions have a disproportionate impact on the audience. First, paraphrase the essence of the question minus the hostility.

> *Q:* "Why do you people always need to pick everything about communication apart?"
> *A:* "You'd like to know why communication professionals are so analytical."

Because hostility usually grows from frustration or fear, acknowledge the concern underlying the question.

> *Q:* "How dare you bureaucrats decide that it's OK to sacrifice *our* children's health! Would you agree to have a chemical dump in *your* neighborhood?"
> *A:* "We appreciate and share your concern for the safety of your children. And that's why this dump will not accept shipments toxic to human beings or the environment."

4. Remember that audience members and you can disagree without hostility. Audiences appreciate speakers who appear open to alternative viewpoints. Just make sure you don't agree with contradictory opinions—your credibility will suffer.

5. When someone asks a question that's inappropriate because it's too specific, too personal, or off the point, offer to discuss the issue with the questioner after the session or during a break. Other polite ways to duck:

> "That's something you ought to discuss with your physician."
> "I don't think I have time to get into that, but there's a good book on the subject called *Creative Dogcatching*. You can probably find it in your library."

6. If someone gives a rambling speech and you don't quite catch what the question is, ask for clarification or restate what you do understand.

"What is the main thing you'd like me to answer?"

"I'm not sure I'm following you. Are you asking me if there's any correlation between astrological signs and success in business?"

7. In the case of a question you answered ten minutes before, don't act annoyed. Unless you're teaching something that must be mastered step by step, you needn't answer it again. Try one of these replies:

"How many times do I have to tell you? We did not trade arms for hostages. . . ." [Just kidding!]

"We talked about that before you came in, so maybe during the break someone else could fill you in."

8. In case silence falls after the call for questions, have a question and answer or two in mind.

"One thing a lot of first-time home buyers wonder about is what will happen if their mortgage application is rejected. Well . . ."

Step forward from the podium to encourage livelier Q & A. Greater friendliness and less formality on your part encourage audience members to speak up.

9. With ridiculous questions, avoid any nonverbal indication that you think the question is dumb—your image with the audience will suffer even if they agree with your disparagement of the questioner. The biggest challenge I ever faced in this regard came after a presentation on speaking skills that I gave at Harvard. A graduate student wearing thick glasses came up to me and said, "I know the cure for the fear of speaking." Sure that he was going to tell me about some cutting-edge discovery, I could hardly wait for him to tell me what it was. "The secret is," he said, "change your underwear right before you speak." It took every ounce of self-control I'd ever had to keep a straight face. "Thanks," I said. "That certainly gives me something to think about."

• I Never Stick to What I've Prepared

If you're one of those people who abandons plans in search of a better way, fine—but for goodness' sake don't do it *in front* of people. Dumping their original idea is an all too common tactic of folks who never felt too swell about their talk in the first place. Occasionally you may be lucky enough to spout some effective rhetoric while you're winging it. Mostly, though, it's irrational to think that an off-the-cuff invention will go better than a planned intention.

Chuck, a financial officer of a training company, felt inadequate speaking at company meetings because many of his colleagues were professional speakers. Though he would prepare or even overprepare his thoughts, he would suddenly decide as he walked up to the lectern to change the talk "just a little." Unfortunately, his "little" changes led to a lot of audience confusion and reinforced Chuck's despair that he didn't have what it took to be an effective speaker. Once Chuck applied the principles below, he recognized that although he wasn't as dynamic as his colleagues, good organization, preparation, and stick-to-itiveness made him the decent speaker he'd hoped to be.

For More Stick-to-itiveness

1. Decide beforehand whether or not you like what you planned. If not, make as many changes as you need to until your ideas feel right.

2. Make final revisions to your talk the night before. Be sure to update facts, figures, and references if necessary.

3. Practice as recommended in "Should I Use Notes, Memorize My Talk, or What?" (page 112) for important presentations.

4. Make this commitment to yourself aloud and in writing:

"I'm satisfied with what I've prepared, and this is what I'll be saying at the meeting tomorrow."

5. You may be especially tempted to abandon ship during the moments before you begin, so add these words to your commitment: "Even though I have the urge to change, it's not in my best interest."

6. During your talk, allow yourself to wander for a spontaneous example, humor, or added perspective. But do not allow any major departure from your original planned outline until you've covered all major points. Visualize a stop sign any time you feel tempted to wander.

7. Reward yourself afterward for maintaining inner and outer control. You have mastered the essence of effective speaking!

• I Was Doing My Best, and They Still Looked Half Asleep

Monica, a real estate agent who was trying to break into the seminar business, came to see me, disappointed about her first performance before a large convention audience. "I was thoroughly prepared, I moved around, I used humor, gestures, and examples," she said. "I know I was dynamic up there, but no matter what I did, they never seemed to wake up. What could I have been doing wrong?" Instead of answering, I asked her a series of questions. What time of day was her session? What was the temperature in the room? Had there been a wild convention party the night before? She learned the hard way that many other factors besides the speaker's delivery influence the reception of the message.

Ideally, every speaker would have an "advance team" that would arrange and control the environment to the speaker's best advantage. But experienced speakers learn to anticipate environmental challenges and maneuver around the less than ideal settings that may be sprung on them.

Stage-Managing for Success

These are environmental factors for speakers to think about.

1. *Air temperature.* Cooler than average is better than too warm, which makes audiences drowsy. But since you as speaker are more keyed up than your listeners, check with audience members before you go around opening windows. When windows won't open or there are no windows, you can sometimes get ventilation by opening doors. If you're stuck with a windowless oven of a room, take more breaks than usual and urge the audience to get some fresh air.

2. *Lights.* Lighting should be appropriate for your purpose.

Bright lights keep an audience alert and focused, while dimmer lighting promotes a cozier atmosphere. Avoid fluorescent lighting whenever possible—it can be harsh and tiring.

3. *Breaks.* Never speak longer than one and a half hours without calling a break. Try to preplan breaks for natural pause points in your program. As the speaker you should be able to tell people where restrooms, refreshments, and so forth are available even if you've never been in that building before, so arrive early and look the place over before you mount the podium. Remember that breaks can serve many purposes besides a stretch and a pit stop: time for networking, buying books, asking questions, and so on.

4. *Decor.* While you usually can't manage a major makeover of the room, you can often make minor adjustments to provide a better backdrop for your talents. If the room contains blackboards, make sure they're erased, and get rid of other distractions such as overflowing trash receptacles. Some speakers bring along fresh flowers and relaxing music on a cassette player to set a mood.

5. *Smoke.* No matter how much of a nicotine fiend you are, don't smoke when you're in the spotlight as the speaker. And don't encourage the audience to do so either since a smoky atmosphere diminishes many people's concentration. A nice way to announce the prohibition might be: "Smokers should feel free to duck out whenever they have the urge."

6. *Audience fatigue.* In an all-day program, the prime fatigue zones hit about forty-five minutes before lunch and midafternoon or about ninety minutes before the end. Break for refreshments or plan more stimulating activities for those times.

7. *Crowdedness.* People may have a hard time being attentive when they're packed in like sardines. If you have an overflow crowd, ask the organizers whether another room is available. At the other extreme, I once found myself scheduled to teach a shyness class in the worst possible environment for shy folks: a large, empty ballroom. Although audiences usually prefer not to sit too close to the speaker, when you have a small crowd in a

big auditorium, enlist some people to move toward the front, and others will as well.

8. *Lectern.* For short people, standard-issue lecterns sometimes present a challenge. Just before Election Day in 1988, I arrived in Newport, Rhode Island, to lecture to personnel administrators and realized that the lectern in the speaking hall would come up to my eyebrows. My hosts brought out a crate for me to stand on, which I declined because it looked dangerous. "What's the matter?" they asked. "Michael Dukakis used this to stand on last week." I have a fantasy of creating a product called "podiums for petites" so that folks who are shorter than average can be seen as well as heard. But in the meantime, if you find yourself in a similar situation, feel free to borrow my solution in Newport: I moved a small table to the front to hold my notes.

• I'm Not Funny, Eloquent, or Interesting—Is There Any Hope for Me?

Yes, if you resist the urge to compare yourself with history's most charismatic speakers (Martin Luther King, Jr., John F. Kennedy). The key to being better than average is finding your own style and refining it, by practicing, adding a technique here and there, and keeping your information fresh. Gloria Steinem, a poised advocate for women's rights, is one who battled a lifelong fear of audiences. In her memoirs she wrote that she has learned three things about public speaking: "There's no right way to speak, only your way; you don't die; and it's worth it."

Ms. Steinem probably became such a successful spokesperson because she was true to her natural way of coming on soft rather than hard and making brave statements without being abrasive. Likewise, Bette Midler's style works for her, and Michael Jackson's for Michael Jackson. Audiences like to feel that the real person, not some fake performer, is up there.

As a speaker, Vice President Dan Quayle suffers from seeming plastic, wooden, or frozen. The best advice for Mr. Quayle would be to find the self that he projected before he hit the big time—an image that was obviously associated with leadership qualities. He and many others need the reassurance of knowing that

GOOD SPEAKERS ARE THEMSELVES AT THEIR BEST.

Using trial and error, aim at finding and being yourself at your best, and you'll attain compliments and confidence as a speaker. Follow these steps to find the speaking style that suits you best.

Finding Your Style

1. Know who you are. Rate yourself by placing an X where you feel you naturally fall along the following personality

dimensions. Since I think I am an expressive speaker, for example, I'd rate myself in the following way along the first dimension:

laid-back. . . . . . . X . . . dramatic

Ask five people who have heard you speak in a situation that felt comfortable for you to rate you as well.

laid-back . . . . . dramatic
informal . . . . . . formal
prepared . . . . . spontaneous
logical . . . . . . emotional
slow-paced . . . . fast-paced
serious . . . . . . humorous
warm . . . . cool
intellectual . . . . down-to-earth
direct . . . . anecdotal

2. Let who you are become your primary style. While you are giving a presentation is not the time to adopt a new personality. If you've never told a joke well, don't try for the first time when you're facing twenty-five or two hundred fifty new faces.

3. Choose characteristics that come naturally to you and amplify them. For example, if you're effortlessly logical, develop lists; if humor comes easily to you, collect jokes and anecdotes. Work on one characteristic at a time.

4. Be aware that you might need to make your style more interesting and varied by purposely developing more characteristics that balance your strengths. For instance, I often help technical people who are geniuses with information to improve their vocal and facial expressiveness and include more anecdotes and examples.

Ultimately, you want the flexibility to be able to incorporate many aspects of style depending on your topic and the audience. For starters, trust that although you may never become one of history's greatest speakers, you may very well become better than good enough.

....

Meeting
Headaches

• I'm Not Sure How to Lead a Meeting

As the leader of a meeting you face a challenge a lot like the task of conducting an orchestra. You set the tempo, watch the pacing, regulate loudness, give appropriate cues, and adjust the balance of contributions to produce a sum that's greater than the parts. As a meeting leader you may not get applause and calls for encores, but when you've done well, *you'll* know you helped the session flow like Toscanini or Leonard Bernstein.

Orchestrating a Meeting

1. Set the context for the meeting:

    "The purpose of tonight's meeting is to decide whether or not the Senior League should take a position on the anti-fur referendum."

2. Introduce each item so discussion is focused:

    "Next we want to come up with ideas for refurbishing the reception area."

3. Encourage group participation:

    "Herb, what are your thoughts about zebra-patterned wallpaper for the corridor?"
    "We haven't heard from any fur owners yet. Jocelyn, Nan, Marlene—?"

4. Summarize frequently:

    "OK, so far we've heard from people who want to stick with a cement ceiling, several who'd like a sky motif, and others who want to reproduce the frescoes in the Sistine Chapel."

5. Keep things moving:

"We've spent enough time now on designer soap. Any other ideas for the bathroom?"

6. Tolerate conflict but don't let it get out of hand:

"Mr. Forsythe, Mrs. Winthrop didn't finish what she had to say. Let's hear her out, and then you can have the floor."
"Let's see, we have a difference of opinion about whether we need paper towels or cloth. Let's go through the pros and cons of each."

7. Make sure that people are physically comfortable, not starving or dying to take a break:

"It's gotten cold and dark. Carlos, would you turn on the lights, and does anyone object if I close the window?"

8. Clearly convey how decisions will be made:

"I'll be getting your input, and then I'll make a decision." (I decide—authoritarian.)
"Let's discuss the proposal for fifteen minutes and then take a vote." (We decide—democratic.)
"I'll be an impartial observer while you reach a consensus." (You decide—laissez-faire.)

Though most of us try to be democratic, it's hard to be both a facilitator and a participant. It is interesting to note that in America's early Continental Congress, the leader of the discussion could not offer an opinion. If he wished to, he'd have to step to the floor and let another member of the Congress take over the meeting.

• What If I Have Only a Minute to Prepare Some Remarks?

Panicking is one option. Another is using the seconds you have to prepare, not despair. Remember that you know something about the topic; otherwise why the heck would anyone ask you to talk about it? What you need to do is convey that knowledge in a manner intelligible to others.

Instant Recipes

When you have a minute or less to prepare:

1. *The Sandwich.* Use ten seconds to prepare an opening and a closing statement (the bread). Use twenty seconds to come up with two to three points (the meat).

Bread: "I'd like to discuss the findings of our readership survey.

Meat: We found that most of our readers were in the 18–24 group; most important, 60 percent were in some phase of educational training; 90 percent had professional ambitions.

Bread: At the next meeting I'll be presenting my recommendations."

2. *Dessert First.* Present a conclusion (dessert) and follow it with two to three supportive points.

Conclusion: "We need to target a more supportive group . . .

Point: because the findings show high educational goals . . .

Point: and concern for a better standard of living."

3. *Dessert Last.* State your points, support, or reasons (two or three) first and your conclusion last. The words *since* and *because* can get you going.

Point: "Since we have ten parents with children under age four . . .

Point: and there's a state grant available . . .

Conclusion: I think we should consider a day-care center at our company."

• I Hold My Opinions In and Then Someone Else Always Says What I Was Going to Say

People who speak up in meetings tend to be perceived as more influential and are more likely to emerge as leaders.

To Let Your Opinions Out

1. Resolve to speak up more whether your input is earth-shattering or not. Set specific goals for your next few meetings and plan to reward yourself for keeping your commitment. If you never speak at meetings, you'll find it easier to start by elaborating on someone else's comment than with a five-minute monologue.

2. Speak up early at every meeting. Contribute within the first few minutes of a discussion even if it's only to agree or ask a question. This warms you up for future contributions.

3. Don't obsess, express. When you have an idea or opinion, allow yourself a maximum of one minute to flesh it out in your head or in notes. Then you're on!

4. Use these starter phrases to break in:

> "I have one additional thought . . ."
> "I'd like to offer an idea."
> "There's another way to look at it."
> "Holly's concept is interesting. Another option would be . . ."
> "May I add something?"

5. Continue this pattern of speaking up often and early for at least five meetings. Soon enough, the next idea that sells will be yours.

• We Waste a Lot of Time at Our Meetings

You have plenty of company. According to numerous surveys, most businesspeople view meetings as boring, unproductive, and a waste of time. (In one poll, 43 percent of executives admitted to having dozed off at a meeting at least once.) Some view meetings as downright unbearable. Is it possible to leave a meeting feeling refreshed, with a heightened sense of teamwork, and ready to take constructive action? Use this diagnostic test and follow up with the necessary cure. There *can* be more to look forward to than danish and coffee.

Your meetings are out of control if:

_____People show up late or not at all.

_____Instead of an agenda, anything and everything comes up.

_____10 percent of the participants do 90 percent of the talking.

_____Most of the topics discussed have no relevance to most of the participants.

_____Things are discussed and discussed and disgust meeting after meeting.

_____There's no procedure for reaching a decision.

_____People use the time for getting paperwork done or for daydreaming about a world without meetings.

_____People wake up only for the name-calling and confrontation.

You can end meeting madness if you:

- Cancel any meeting you don't really need.
- Call a meeting *only* when the input of the group is necessary for discussion and constructive action.
- Use other communication methods (memo, telephone) for routine announcements.

- Create and distribute an agenda several days in advance.
- Include participants' concerns by inviting all beforehand to suggest topics for discussion.
- Break down the agenda by the time allotted for each topic of discussion.
- Consider having certain participants attend only relevant parts of the meeting.
- Include introductory and concluding statements for each agenda item.
- Let participants know how and when a decision will be made: "Let's hear your ideas for our fund-raising project. Next Tuesday, the executive board will vote on them."
- Keep meetings as short as possible.
- Take frequent breaks, about once every hour and a half during a long meeting.
- Brush up on listening and group leadership skills (see "What Do I Do When the Meeting Gets Off Track?" on page 162).
- Don't forget the goodies—try juice and fruit for a change from coffee and doughnuts.

WARNING

Exposure to too many meetings can be dangerous to your company's health. Stick to a moderate meeting dosage.

• We Never Make Any Decisions at Our Meetings

According to research on meetings recently reported in *The New York Times:*

- Good decision making requires a special mix of people. One study found that the most productive groups included members who were strong in intelligence, creativity, and practicality. Groups lacking one or more of these ingredients faltered or overlooked flaws in proposed actions.
- Though they're the ones who call meetings, two hundred executives surveyed estimated that 20 to 30 percent of the issues discussed in meetings could have been better handled by phone or memo.
- Many meeting participants are just wasting their time. Topics discussed have nothing to do with their jobs, nor can they contribute productively to discussion.

The first decision, then, is whether the group is the best format for finding solutions. If you believe that group members can contribute useful input, look next at the group's decision-making process.

To Get Somewhere in a Meeting

1. Set realistic goals regarding what can and can't be decided. State exactly what needs to be decided at the meeting when a topic is raised.

"Today we need to brainstorm titles for Paul McNeely's bird-watching book and decide on the best one."

2. Be clear on how much time you'll spend on discussion

and how decisions will be made. State this at the outset to avoid misunderstandings later. See "I'm Not Sure How to Lead a Meeting" (page 153) for the three major decision-making styles and their pros and cons.

3. Keep it moving. In a group of peers, appoint a leader or facilitator to make sure all possibilities are heard and discussion stays on track.

4. Analyze the problem and review necessary background information.

> "Let's look at the titles of previous birding books."
>
> "What are bird-watchers looking for in a book these days?"
>
> "What's unique about Paul's book?"

Note: Prevent obstacles at this stage by having relevant information at hand. Someone ought to have already looked up all the past bird-watching titles!

5. Generate solutions. List as many ideas as possible without coming to a solution too quickly. Remember, with input from different sources, a combination of three ideas may prove better than one. Stay on the lookout, though, for:

- the most powerful people generating all the ideas or knocking the ones others have brought up
- quiet group members keeping ideas to themselves

6. Choose the best solution, using the decision-making method previously announced. You may need to select the most promising options first for a vote.

> "We've heard suggestions for three titles: *Bird-watching Made Simple, Bird-watching in a Week,* and *Birds in Your Backyard.* Please note your first and second choices on a slip of paper and pass it forward."

7. Once a decision is made, make sure someone is responsible for implementing it.

> "John, will you make sure that the marketing and production group is notified of our decision?"

• What Do I Do When the Meeting Gets Off Track?

If you are leading the meeting, it's your job to manage meandering. It is not comfortable to be a human stop sign, but it can be a necessity. Remember, though, that business meetings often serve a networking and social purpose in addition to the official purpose, so don't crack the whip every time your group wanders. The effective leader allows for chitchat, tangents, and new topics while making sure that there is a sense of purpose, focus, and control.

To Manage Meeting Meandering

1. *Distribute an agenda.* This helps people keep in mind what needs to be discussed and accomplished.

2. *Be flexible.* Your decision to get things back on track depends on how much time there is to spare and the degree of consensus regarding the importance of new topics raised. Let's say you're discussing the topic of your next Christmas party. The idea of donating food to the homeless in lieu of the party comes up and wins a groundswell of support. The wise leader would not say, "Let's get back to the Christmas party. We didn't come here to talk about the homeless."

3. *Use tact in lassoing the group back.* Acknowledge what is on the floor and the importance of switching gears.

> "I love talking about the game, too, but we need to discuss next year's training budget by the end of the meeting."

> "The new system for tuition reimbursement is an important topic. Let's bring it up next Wednesday. Today, let's focus on modifying the health-care package."

Tip: Allow three minutes of getting off target before you start swinging the rope.

If there is no designated leader, gently remind the group of what remains to be settled. You might feel uncomfortable, but in the long run people will give you credit for sticking your neck out. Suggest a focus that will move important business to resolution.

"I know people have strong opinions about the vice president's remarks, but we still need to decide what to put in the report. How about if we sum up the pros and cons of each of the options people have mentioned?"

• How Do I Excuse Myself to Go to the Restroom?

Long meetings were not invented to accommodate normal human functions. Sensitive meeting planners schedule plenty of "stretches." I'll never forget what one participant wrote on a feedback form after a program I gave. When asked what her favorite part of the session was, she wrote, "The breaks!"

If it's possible, make a pit stop before the meeting. But if you have to leave, here are a few strategic ways to stage an exit:

1. *The graceful exit:* Stand with confidence and whisper or quietly say, "Excuse me," as you open and close the door without another peep.

2. *The invisible exit:* Inch your chair to a more comfortable position for leaving and wait until a topic comes up that doesn't concern you. Then get up and move swiftly and quietly, looking only at the door.

3. *The power exit:* This exit assumes that other colleagues have the same need as you, but they're afraid to speak up. Use this exit only if you're the leader or a respected group member. A power exit consists of saying one of the following at a pause in the meeting:

> "We'll do better thinking after a ten-minute time-out."
> "What do you say we take a break?"
> "It's been two hours. It's time for a stretch."

Usually you'll be appreciated for this. As one of my wise colleagues once announced at a meeting, "The mind can only absorb what the behind can endure."

• How Do I Handle Difficult People in Meetings?

For effective meetings, participants must be able to tackle the agenda without angering one another. If the leader can't recognize and control disruptive personality types, inefficiency and friction result. Reuben, head of the program committee for a large nonprofit organization, enjoyed his responsibilities except for one tough obstacle, Trisha. She had lost out to Reuben for head of the committee but took charge anyway by putting down everyone's ideas and arguing openly with Reuben about his "unassertive leadership." Group members started complaining about her presence. To preserve the health of his committee, Reuben needed to learn about:

Meeting Manglers and How to Manage Them

Type 1: The Bull
Identifying characteristic: runs down people's ideas.
   To keep the bull penned in:

- Give him some authority (like being head of a project), which may lessen his need to take over by force.
- Don't lock horns by replying with hostility; instead, act and sound calm.
- Find some value in his ideas and rephrase them to the group in a less threatening way.

   The bull: "Sue's idea to bring in Oliver North as a speaker is absurd. He's too political for this town, and he charges ten thousand bucks."
   Leader: "So you think North is too expensive and political. Sue, what's your reaction to those concerns?"

P.S. Reuben tried these strategies with Trish and found that though people still couldn't stand her, they felt he was more in control as a leader. He also said that when he gave her a bit more power in the group, Trish told Reuben his leadership skills had improved!

Type 2: The Astronaut
Identifying characteristic: speaks tangentially, never on track.
  To ground the astronaut:

- Avoid responding to her tangents. Express appreciation and get right back on the topic.
- If she gets others involved in discussion, just say, "Though this is interesting, can we get back to the major problem we need to solve?"
- Astronauts do well when asked specific questions such as, "Nell, do you think we need another receptionist in the front lobby?" instead of open questions such as, "What do you think we need for the front lobby?"

Type 3: The Joker
Identifying characteristic: sees every meeting as an opportunity to get attention.
  If you want the joker to get serious:

- Ask in advance if he can help you out with presenting data, overheads, and so forth.
- Ask his advice on how to make meetings more productive. He might behave as he does because he feels time isn't used well anyway.
- Avoid giving false cues that you're being entertained and explicitly convey your desire for seriousness with "Let's get serious" or "OK, enough fooling around."

Type 4: The Blob
Identifying characteristic: just sits there, watching, watching, watching.

To jog the blob:

- Try gently drawing her out: "What are your thoughts about that, Nancy?" (If she is supershy, ask privately in advance if that's OK.)
- Give her a small but significant task to perform in the group that forces more interaction (being in charge of a sign-up list, collecting reports, and so on).
- Touch base more one on one between meetings to get her thoughts on how she thinks the group is going and how meetings could be more useful to her.

··········

Tough Situations

• I Get Upset When I'm Criticized

It's difficult to hear and to respond appropriately to others' opinions about your personality, your actions, or your work. Chances are you either fall apart or fight back instead of listening and deciding whether X's point has any real merit.

Instead of cringing and cowering at your next feedback session, use it as an opportunity to shine. Actually invite constructive criticism. The three-step method explained below will help you remain composed no matter how bad the news.

Murray tended to fight back when criticized. He argued vehemently when his boss told him he needed to develop better leadership and organizational skills. Murray contended that those were two of his strengths. Not only was his boss not convinced, six months later he repeated his previous criticisms along with a new one: doesn't take criticism well. To keep his job, Murray asked me how he could avoid another confrontation with his boss. *The Three Ps* enabled him to keep his cool and impress his boss.

Paraphrase: Show your boss you hear her concerns clearly by repeating them in different words. ("You're concerned about our efficiency in collecting bills.")

Prompt: Gather all the information you can about how the situation or your skills could use improvement. That's right, ask for criticism! ("What do you think could be improved in our collecting methods?")

Provide solutions: Maintain control by being the first to offer a constructive solution. ("I'd like to examine several new collection strategies this week. After that, I'd like for us to meet to decide which one or ones will work best.")

It's possible to turn even tricky evaluation sessions to your advantage. Remember *The Three Ps*—*P*araphrase, *P*rompt, *P*rovide solutions—and you'll withstand criticism with confidence.

• Is There a Way to Give Criticism Without Hurting Someone's Feelings?

Since people are sensitive to others' opinions of them and often resent even a polite request for change, it makes sense to evaluate whether or not you should offer criticism in the first place. So first see if you can answer yes to most of the following:

Critical Questions

- Is the person capable of changing?
- Will the criticism help your well-being or the person's well-being?
- Is it your job or responsibility to offer the particular criticism?
- Can you share your concern without sarcasm or anger? (Because you surely won't be heard otherwise.)

Once you have determined that the role of critic suits you, use the *Plus-Minus-Plus* (+ − +) method to help both of you feel more comfortable.

Plus (+): Say something positive first. An honest, specific comment is best.

Minus (−): Describe what's bugging you without blame, putdowns, sarcasm, or strong emotion. State the troublesome consequence of the problem.

> "I can't study when the music is blaring."
> "More formal dress would add to our credibility."
> "I get a headache when there's smoke near me."

Plus (+): End by again saying something positive about the conversation or expressing appreciation for efforts to change.

For example, Steve is annoyed with Craig for not doing his fair share on a company proposal.

· *Plus* (+): "Craig, I think we did a great job together on the Data International report."

Minus (−): "I've been working overtime on the Collins proposal. I think if we divide up the work equally, it will go more smoothly."

Plus (+): "Thanks for working this out. I'm sure things will run easily from now on."

• Should I Stretch the Truth at a Job Interview?

Lying to get a job isn't very smart, whether you're inflating your skills ("I'm totally fluent in French" when you only studied it for two years in high school), your experience ("I've written dozens of press releases" when you only retyped your boss's), or your willingness to do the job ("Sure, I'll relocate to Siberia"). But if you regard selling yourself and singing your own praises as stretching the truth, then change your way of thinking. Let your true talents and potential shine during an interview. With these guidelines, you can tell the truth and still get the job.

Talking Yourself Into the Job

1. *Know how to talk about yourself.* Prepare and practice talking about your accomplishments, hitting on these four points:

- The substance of your accomplishments: "I supervised five salespeople."
- Benefit to your old employer: "I increased productivity 20 percent."
- Benefit to you personally: "I gained problem-solving skills and learned how to lead groups."
- Benefit to prospective employer: "I think I can offer you the directive management style you're looking for."

2. *Answer questions your way.* Though you can't control what the interviewer will ask, you can control the content and tone of your answers. Remember to talk about what you *did* do, what you *are* doing, and what you *will* do. Never voluntarily mention what you *haven't* done, *won't* do, or *can't* do. Display confidence by using strong verbs such as:

"I *achieved* [a 20 percent increase in productivity]."
"I *developed* [a five-year marketing plan]."
"I *initiated* [a company newsletter]."

• How Should I Sit During a Job Interview?

Your goal is to strike a pose in which you look influential and impressive but not more influential and impressive than the interviewer. In other words, the "right way" to sit and move is always relative to the cues provided by the person sizing you up. You can adapt yourself to the interviewer's style by noting how he or she looks and matching that behavior closely.

Karen was eager to land a fast-track corporate-law position but had failed to be invited back for a second interview at a prestigious firm. While discussing her disappointment, Karen remembered that while the partners interviewing her had spread out on comfortable chairs and sofas, in shirt-sleeves, she had sat "like a matron" in a straight-back chair, with her hands folded on her lap. Her decision to be formal, which she thought would make her appear older, probably backfired in this case. We practiced adapting to different interviewer styles until Karen said she was feeling more like a chameleon than a matron— a good indication of progress.

Positions of Influence

For job interviews and other hot seats:

1. *Influential people look relaxed.* Avoid remaining in the same posture throughout the whole interview. Find a posture you can rely on to begin with, such as hands relaxed on your lap or on the sides of the chair. Then change it according to the next two tips.

2. *Influential people take up space.* Watch out for squishing, scrunching, or hunching in a chair. If given a choice, pick the seat that will make you look best. If the interviewer uses energetic gestures and shifts posture frequently, feel free to do so as

well. One warning note, though: No matter how relaxed the interviewer seems, don't spread yourself or your things on his or her desk—that's too relaxed and may make the interviewer feel invaded.

3. *Influential people watch the other guy.* Your interviewer will give you plenty of cues about how comfortable to make yourself, so don't go in with preconceived notions. Use the technique called "mirroring" to subtly adjust your postures to the interviewer's. This will build a sense of trust and rapport between you.

If she leans forward slightly, you lean forward slightly.

If he crosses or uncrosses his legs, you can follow.

If she averts her eyes for a few seconds while speaking, you can do the same.

Note: Don't go overboard with mirroring. Even if your department head often sits with his feet up on his desk, your feet should remain on the floor!

• My Boss Is Always Bugging Me

No matter how great the job, your creativity decreases and hostility increases when you feel every move is being monitored by the boss. If you're sure you'd do a better job if your boss weren't clucking and pecking at you all the time, it's probably worth trying to influence his style.

Colby, a laboratory technician, respected his supervisor Cynthia's judgment when administered in proper doses. Colby came to see me after Cynthia's constant prodding reached the point where she'd follow him to the men's room and wait until he came out to finish her comments. Though Colby knew Cynthia was under pressure to produce some dramatic results soon, he found himself wanting to avoid the lab he had once thought of as his second home. Colby wondered how he could get Cynthia off his case without causing an explosion in the lab.

To Get Your Boss Off Your Back

1. *Get to him first.* Why is he on your case, anyway (needs to feel in control, concerned about your performance, nothing else to do, thinks it's his responsibility)? Once you figure out his motivation, try to check in with him before he checks in with you by giving him an update, asking advice, or getting a list of "to dos" for the day. Colby calmed Cynthia down somewhat by reporting on his progress every morning and afternoon and reminding her that the lab still had five and a half months to come up with something before the next grant deadline.

2. *Tell him how you prefer to be supervised.* During a performance review or a meeting initiated by you, ask if it would be useful for him to know how you best accomplish tasks. Then be clear about your requirements.

> "It would help me a lot if we checked in with each other at the beginning and end of the day." .

"I'd be most productive if I could wait until the first phase of the experiment is over before giving you a full report."

3. *Give feedback tactfully.* Let the boss know how over-monitoring affects you. Use the *Plus-Minus-Plus* technique described in "Is There a Way to Give Criticism Without Hurting Someone's Feelings?" on page 172.

Plus: "You always have a lot of great suggestions, Cynthia."

Minus: "I do find that when I need to touch base with you five times a day, it interrupts my concentration and it's harder for me to work efficiently."

Plus: "I really do value your insights and hope we can find a way to check in with each other every other day or so."

4. *Develop immunity to his presence.* If the above ideas don't work and you want to remain in your position, shift your attitude. Accept that the interference and annoyance come with the job. When Cynthia continued to nag Colby a little more than he liked, he would tell himself, "She's being a nuisance, but I can get back to work as soon as I calmly tell her my agenda for the next few hours."

• I Can't Stand Having to Sell (a Product, Service, or Myself)

This is a common complaint from people who are proud of their profession (accountants, administrators, and artists head the list) but find that in the real world the ability to do a job well is not always enough. You also have to sell your expertise, and someone has to buy. To some proud professionals, "sales" is synonymous with "sleaze." In order to become comfortable with selling, assure yourself that you have something to offer that will add to somebody's well-being. To test this, answer the following question in fifteen words or less: What is beneficial about your product or service? Example: cat and dog health insurance. Benefits: makes owners feel more secure, helps sick pets.

If you can't answer this question sincerely and clearly, then no wonder selling feels like an ordeal!

Once you think of the benefits of what you are offering, it should be easier to think of selling as forming a relationship with a client in which you both benefit. Ed Pierce, a phenomenally successful portrait and wedding photographer in the Washington, D.C., area, lectures nationally to other photographers who would be happy to have one-tenth of his business. Ed has evolved a nonmanipulative selling style that puts clients at ease and helps build business for the long run. He advocates letting the client come naturally to a decision without being pressured. For people who feel as Ed does, the partnership or *T-E-A-M* approach may be the way to communicate.

The *T-E-A-M* approach involves these steps:

Trust building, the foundation for mutually comfortable business relationships. You approach the client in an open, genuine spirit about what you can offer.

"I was hoping we could meet to talk about ways my company might help you modernize your office systems."

Engaging the client. For a mutually beneficial partnership, you need to find out what specifically the other party needs and how your product or service might fit into his world.

"In order to best meet your needs, I'd like to get to know how your current system is working. What's been the response so far? How satisfied are you? How do you think the system could be enhanced?"

Applying. Based on what you've heard, present an overview of what you can offer, with the most focus on concerns and issues your prospective client has raised. A canned presentation will not succeed.

"Our initial customer service support package might be the solution for the front-line problems that you mentioned. Would you like me to describe our different alternatives?"

Mutual action and agreement. In the final phase you and the client agree on the next best step. He will decide whether or not to buy based on many factors—most important, how great he perceives his need to be for your product or service and how well you've communicated that you can meet his need.

"I think I have a good understanding of the kind of quality you're looking for. A good plan may be to try the system for three months and then reevaluate."
"Of the three different options I've described, which do you think will work for you?"

While the *T-E-A-M* approach may not always win you the sale, it will keep you happy with how you played the game.

• How Do I Tell Someone She's Not Up to Snuff?

First off, decide to do it. Too many managers wait until a formal evaluation to drop the bad news, leaving employees alienated and angry. Sure, you don't want to hurt someone's feelings, but in the long run it is far more hurtful to let poor incompetent Inez bumble on without guidance. Remember that if part of your job is to help others do *their* job better, withholding criticism is unfair.

Dr. Kavanaugh, a busy gastroenterologist, didn't want to tell his office manager, Charlotte, that her billing methods were a disaster; office income had decreased 20 percent since she took over. Dr. Kavanaugh said he would rather let the problem sit because Charlotte had just moved to a new apartment and was visiting her ailing mother in a nearby nursing home every lunchtime. But after some discussion, Dr. Kavanaugh admitted that everyone would be better off if he took the situation in hand as soon as possible. Undoubtedly it would cause some short-term grief, but in the long run, relief.

Prescription for Getting Staff Into Shape Gently

1. *Resolve.* Once you are convinced that improvement is necessary for the employee and the office, commit yourself to set aside time to talk within a week. No longer!

2. *Praise first.* If you can offer genuine praise about her skills and manner, do so. This will put the rougher stuff in context.

3. *Two-step discussion of concern.* (a) Describe the behavior that's your concern. Be specific. (b) Describe the impact it's having on you, others, or the office.

(a) "I've noticed that the billing is done in a random fashion and only every other week instead of every week." (b) "That's brought a 20 percent decrease in our income over the past couple of months."

4. *The prescription.* Say what needs to happen. Always talk about what you would like to see, not what you don't see.

"We need to work out a billing plan that is efficient and that we can feel comfortable with."

Give your employee time to respond. Expect some surprise, defensiveness, or resentment.

5. *The plan.* Work out a plan for supporting her efforts to shape up, and agree on a time when you'll both review the situation.

6. *If it can't be worked out.* If you've given her a clear description of what needs to happen but it doesn't happen within the time frame you agreed on, it may be best to acknowledge the mismatch between what the job requires and what this employee can do. There is a time for everything, and this may be the time to let go.

• My Colleague Always Stands Too Close

Each of us has a set of unspoken rules about how close or how far from others we like to sit, stand, and talk. Violations of our personal space can provoke intense discomfort. The rules themselves come mainly from our cultural and family backgrounds. One client, who grew up in a cold New England family where she and her parents always sat a table leaf apart during dinner, had a hard time adjusting to her husband's family, who huddled and cuddled for what she described as "no good reason."

Through body language and manipulation of objects—the length of our desk, where we place our chair or couch, which seat we choose at the board meeting—we unconsciously broadcast our preferences to others. As we get to know a colleague, we adjust our separate space requirements to interact comfortably as a team. Usually our boundaries are respected, but every once in a while, along comes a Space Invader.

The attack of the Space Invader occurs because:

1. The Space Invader is oblivious to or does not know how to accommodate your boundaries.

2. You are not giving a clear enough message about your space requirements. Mark, an account executive in the travel industry, complained that his secretary would practically nuzzle him in the hallway. When I asked what he did in response, he said, "The polite thing, of course—I looked straight into her eyes!"

3. The Space Invader is attacking to express dominance or power. Think of the expression, "She's breathing down my neck." Or picture a military drill instructor chewing out a recruit while standing almost nose to nose.

To Stop the Space Invader in His Tracks

1. Situate yourself so that a piece of furniture or an object is always between you. Marian, a graduate student, had a hard time coping with a famous professor in her department who retained some of the customs of his old-world background. Every time she spoke to him after class, he would stand so close she'd instinctively take a step backward. He would step toward her again, she'd step back, and they'd be slowly dancing around the room until she was backed up against a blackboard. When Marian clasped her notebook against her chest, however, it felt like a shield protecting her, and she had an easier time standing her ground.

2. Change your spatial relationship to suit you, not the invader. Jan's boss liked to stand behind her with his hand on her chair whenever he went over the day's schedule. It made her skin crawl, she said. Jan learned to get up whenever he came into her office, arrange two chairs three feet apart, and invite him to sit down before interacting.

3. If efforts to create more distance don't work, it may be time for a more direct presentation of your concern. Say what you need in order to be more comfortable. Make a positive statement first if you're concerned about injuring the invader's feelings:

> "Jerry, our morning reviews are helpful. You have a way of literally coming too close for comfort, though. I'd feel much better with a few more inches between us. Thanks."

For your reference, here are the standard American comfort zones:

Comfortable formal distance: three to six feet apart.
Comfortable acquaintance distance: two to three feet apart.
Average close friend distance: 1½ feet apart.
Still closer friend distance: eight to twelve inches apart.
Intimate friend or lover distance: six inches or less apart.

• How Do I Tell Someone He's Doing Something Annoying or Inappropriate?

Calling bothersome behavior to someone's attention is difficult. You feel as if you're insulting him, encroaching on a small chunk of his identity, or inhibiting his personal freedom ("They're my nails, and I'll chomp on them if I want to!"). Yet because weird, maddening, or disgusting habits are not usually displayed to bug you, you're probably doing the other person a big favor when you tell him something no one else will.

Jeannette felt uncomfortable around her new colleague. Martin was a nice enough guy, but his habit of adjusting his tie every fifteen seconds was annoying to her and clients. His behavior might be understandable in a stand-up comic but seemed out of place in an executive search firm. Jeannette, a reserved woman, asked me in some embarrassment how she could say what needed to be said. I agreed this was a delicate communication mission. Fortunately, the tips below helped. Startled to hear that he was touching his tie all the time, Martin sheepishly thanked Jeannette and told her to signal him whenever he was doing it again.

How to Get People to Get Rid of Annoying Behavior

1. Admit that what you want to tell them is a little annoying, embarrassing, personal, difficult, and so on. This way you'll seem more like a pal than a pest.

2. Acknowledge that what you'll be talking about is just a habit, not something he does on purpose. This way you help him save face.

3. Say directly what you have observed. Avoid hemming and hawing. Practice if you need to. Example:

"I notice that when we're with clients you eat with your fingers."

4. Say what impact the habit has on others if you need to make a stronger point.

". . . and I think it gives the impression that our firm isn't very sophisticated."

5. If your colleague doesn't immediately make a self-suggestion (most people will say something like, "Thanks, I'll watch that"), *you* can offer a suggestion or ask what you could do to help.

"I don't want to be a pain, but is there a way I could signal you if it happens when we're with clients?"

• If I've Said Something Ten Zillion Times, How Can I Not Seem Bored?

Saying the same thing constantly can make you feel robotic, hypnotic, or in the case of a telephone operator who estimated she went through the same spiel twenty-four thousand times a year, a bit psychotic.

Stage actors who successfully play one role over and over again know how to maximize pleasure in sameness. The late Yul Brynner, who will forever be the King of Siam in *The King and I*, relished each and every one of his 4,625 performances. Reaching beyond the words and music to create a bond with each new audience seems to be the essential motivator for experienced speakers as well as stage actors. One seasoned motivational speaker told me that her best moments come after the point at which she knows the content, wording, and timing of a presentation in her sleep. Then she feels free to wander from her planned agenda, to respond flexibly to audience questions, and to add spontaneous humor and comments. Though it is unrealistic to think we'll feel euphoric the 742nd time we tell a customer how to get to the restroom in our shopping mall, there are ways—

To Manage Repetition Burnout

1. Visualize a peaceful or enjoyable image as you say the words. One young city tour bus guide visualizes what he describes as "romantic encounters" as he guides 250 people a day on the same route—five days a week.

2. Focus on the audience, not the words. Allow time for questions that can help you break out of a routine and come across more personably to the audience. Debbie, the assistant director of an art museum, taught art appreciation to seven-

teen groups a week. She told me that she loved art but felt her classes were getting routine. When Debbie found ways to let the kids comment on paintings and sculptures and ask plenty of amusing questions, her malaise disappeared.

3. Pay attention to your delivery. How about putting energy into vocal variety, speech clarity, and influential nonverbal behaviors? In fact, if you pick any skill from other sections of this book and practice for a week, you'll feel more interest in your spiel and become a finer speaker to boot.

4. Know when to quit. If, after trying these techniques, you still feel monotony mouth is on the verge of killing you, it's time for a rest or perhaps a permanent vacation from that job.

• How Can I Break a Date Without Damaging a Relationship?

As comedian Woody Allen has quipped, "Eighty percent of life is showing up." Eighty percent shouldn't be taken lightly! As well intentioned as your excuse may be, the consequences for your broken date may include lost time, lost income, or lost momentum in your business or personal relationship.

Status and power play a role. The more highly placed person is allowed a lot more leeway in making and breaking appointments before suffering obvious consequences. Few of us would cancel a date with the Queen of England or Paul McCartney. And if they proposed rescheduling, it would undoubtedly be, "Fine, fine, at your convenience, Your Majesty, Your Beatleship."

No matter what your power or position, though, a *pattern* of breaking appointments damages your credibility and reputation. Do your best to keep your appointments, then, but if you absolutely must cancel:

1. *Make your excuses as truthful as possible.* Do not say, for example, that you had a family emergency in Montreal if there is any possibility you'll meet your canceled colleague at the Minimart in Minneapolis.

2. *Make your excuses as tactful as possible.* Never imply you're bowing out because something better came along. Blame circumstances beyond your control: an emergency, someone else's mistakes, forces of nature, another person's needs or demands.

> *Untactful:* "The Governor asked me to come in to talk about my project on Wednesday, and I completely forgot we'd decided on a lunch meeting that day."
>
> *Tactful:* "Jim, the company set up a mandatory project meeting all day on Wednesday, and that's the day we were going to meet for lunch."

3. *Acknowledge inconvenience briefly. Suggest alternatives swiftly.*

> *No:* "Gee, I'm sorry. If it weren't for the Governor, I'd love to see you on Wednesday. But maybe we can find another time. Got any ideas?"
>
> *Yes:* "I'm really sorry about messing up your schedule. Could we move our lunch to the following Wednesday?"

To show that you value the relationship, you might even send a note of thanks for the reschedule.

Warning: Even when you follow these guidelines, breaking appointments more than twice in a row can break a relationship beyond repair. Most people can't help taking it personally when they're put off so often.

• How Can I Persuade Someone Who Argues With Everything?

Every person you meet has a unique perspective comprised of thousands of opinions and values shaped, formed, molded, and maybe twisted by their particular combination of experiences, parents, siblings, teachers, friends, jobs, culture, religion, home locations, sitters, pets, and so forth. So when you're trying to convince a person, you're up against quite a well-formed personal universe. To persuade effectively you must communicate in a way that allows your potential convincee to accommodate you and your viewpoints. To the extent that your conversational partner experiences an "alien" idea as "not to be allowed in," your communication will fail. To the extent that she perceives you as a "helpful visitor from another planet," you're in.

After a dozen years of working together, Trudy decided to figure out why she and her lab partner, Carole, argued over every little thing and why each thought the other was stubborn and selfish. Trudy came to see me after a disagreement over the ideal lighting for their lab resulted in a week of bickering and slammed doors. Though Carole refused to come in for communication mediation, she did agree to listen to the suggestions Trudy gleaned from our meetings. While the lab hasn't turned into Shangri-la, Trudy confided that their disagreements now are mere tiffs, not week-long battles. And as Trudy has learned to express her needs directly and without hostility, Carole even offered Trudy a ride home once when Trudy's car broke down.

To Persuade the Unpersuadable

1. *Look for a kernel of agreement.* Find something in your conversational partner's point of view you can really agree with before presenting your side.

"I can see how having the shades down helps you concentrate on your work."

2. *Avoid "but" words.* Words such as *but, however,* and *unless* signal that you're about to argue back. That will just make her disagree more. Why hold up a red flag to a bull? Instead:

"I feel claustrophobic without being able to look out the window."

3. *Go gently, gently.* Try not to state your opinion directly. You will lock horns. Go for softeners such as *might* and *could* instead of *have to* and *should.*

Bad: "We have to answer the telephone before the third ring."

Better: "It might be good for our work if we both tried to pick up the telephone before the third ring."

4. *Don't overreact to his arguments or skepticism.* Show confidence by continually using summaries and paraphrases to show you've heard his viewpoint.

"You're saying that you feel uncomfortable when you can't see outside."

5. *Don't get argumentative back.* Settle for one stressed-out human being rather than two. Raising your voice or using hostile, blaming language wins you nothing but alienation.

Bad: "You're a real jerk to make a federal case out of a window shade."

Better: "Let's see if we can come up with a compromise. How about putting up a divider between your desk and the window?"

Remember: You can't make someone a less argumentative person. You *can* make sure you're not the one she's arguing with.

• I Never Know What to Say to a Friend Who Just Lost Someone

Many people know they ought to offer condolences and want to, but they're frozen by the fear of saying the wrong thing. Yet saying nothing can cause greater pain. Rose, a high school principal and a widow, once told me about her friend Helene, who vanished from her life when Rose's husband was ill (he later died). Since Rose had once heard Helene announce, "I just can't deal with sickness and death," Rose wasn't surprised. "She'd better be able to deal with losing a few friends, then," Rose said to me. When Helene did come around again, Rose wasn't willing to resume their former relationship; the lack of compassionate communication when it was needed had wounded her too much.

Some understanding of the psychology of grief and comfort can help you communicate as you ought to.

What You Need to Know About Consoling Someone

1. Time passes slowly when grief is fresh. Condolences will be most comforting if you offer them as soon as possible after you hear the news.

2. Eloquently worded sentiments aren't necessary. Two simple words are enough: "I'm sorry." They accomplish wonders out of proportion to their length, so say them. A somber expression and a light touch reinforce the human contact accomplished by the words.

3. Listening can provide as much or more solace than talking. Don't fire questions at a mourner, no matter how curious you are to know how and why the death occurred; nonverbally indicate your willingness to listen, for example, by waiting

around silently. If the person begins to talk and becomes upset, don't minimize the loss by saying things like, "Maybe it was for the best" or "You'll have other children." Just listen. Talking helps the bereaved person move through the stages of grief.

4. Actions can be a greater boon than words. After a brief expression of sympathy, ask if there is anything you can do to help, such as bringing over food, taking care of the baby, notifying out-of-town friends.

It is rare that simple communications have the chance to do so much good. Once you witness the effect of prompt, plain consolation, you'll need less courage to extend kindness the next time.

• Why Do Some People Talk So Much, and How Can You Politely Shut Them Up?

Voluminous verbalization is usually a sign that the speaker is uncomfortable in general or uncomfortable around you in the specific situation. Like many consultants, I've noticed that some clients talk all the way through their first session, without even pausing for my feedback or advice. The second session, however, I see a different personality. Nonstop talk helps them maintain a sense of control and security in an unfamiliar environment. If you're patient, then, certain overtalkative folks will quiet down on their own.

Indeed, the most polite way to get someone to talk less is paradoxical: Listen more!

Since excess talking is most often due to discomfort or insecurity, your first tactic is to help your loquacious conversational partner feel appreciated and listened to. Express interest in her ideas, compliment, and show agreement. When you notice her rate of speech slowing down and the number of questions increasing, you'll know you've made headway. If after ten minutes your strategy has had little impact, however, resign yourself to a long night as a good listener. Other strategies, such as withdrawing your attention, redirecting the topic of conversation, or ending the conversation, may also work but are not as polite.

People with certain learning disabilities have a "filtering problem"—difficulty in separating relevant from irrelevant information—so they say everything. With poor filterers you need to redirect the conversation gently and specifically: "I'm afraid we're getting off on a tangent. Let's get back to the pros and cons of Rae's proposal."

By the way, though women have a reputation as the gabbier sex, studies show that in mixed groups males hold the floor much more than women, and the topics they introduce are more likely to be discussed—as long as the sexes stay in the same room, that is.

• How Do I Use an Interpreter?

When doing business overseas, all too many Americans confuse interpreters by mumbling, using American sports metaphors, or extending courtesies to the interpreter, not the foreign boss. Here are some tips for maximizing the chances of your message getting across courteously and accurately when an interpreter is translating your words to someone else, and someone else's words to you.

To Avoid Business Being Lost in Translation

1. Remember whom you are addressing. It is *not* the interpreter. If you are speaking with Mr. Ayamoto, maintain eye contact with him, and address him directly. Say, "May I order three thousand of these now?" not "Ask him if I may order three thousand of these now."

2. Slow down your normal pace of speaking and pause after every two or three sentences. Otherwise the interpreter may miss, forget, condense, or mangle parts of what you have said.

3. Avoid slang, irony, sarcasm, and jokes, all of which don't travel well. Instead of translating a joke, one interpreter in China reportedly said, "The foreigner has just told a complicated joke. Please laugh here."

4. Don't assume that someone speaking to you through an interpreter understands no English. Ms. Vasquez may merely lack good pronounciation, confidence, a specialized vocabulary, or fluency. Thus, don't say anything to your colleagues or the interpreter that you wouldn't want your foreign counterpart to hear.

5. When numbers form an important part of your message, write them down if you don't see the interpreter doing so. Even

better, bring prepared handouts in both languages to foreign meetings or negotiations.

6. Don't draw conclusions from your counterpart's body language or gestures. A nod of the head in response to your question may mean, "Yes, I see what he is saying," not "Yes, I agree with what you have said." Ask for explicit verbal confirmation of what you believe was agreed on.

7. Since communication through an interpreter takes at least twice as long, save everyone's sanity and patience by saying only what absolutely must be said, as directly and clearly as possible.

• I Want My Boss to Know My Accomplishments Without Blowing My Own Horn

I like to say that the wheel that *speaks* gets the grease. Although you might be able to concoct a plan to get someone else to pass your news on to your boss, generally you'll need to speak for yourself. It is possible to let your boss know what you've achieved without bragging, boasting, or broadcasting. Think of it from your organization's standpoint: Any feather in your cap is a feather in everyone's. The wise boss appreciates your accomplishments because they reflect his talent as a guide, mentor, or watchdog. If you can shift your perspective from yourself to the good of the organization as a whole, you won't hang back from sharing your triumphs.

Bonnie, an innovative psychotherapist, developed a tape program that helped clients break addictive habits. She was reluctant to tell her clinic director about her program's success for fear that it would look as if she were trying to show up her colleagues. Finally she left her boss a note along with a tape and case study. He wrote back in big letters, WHY DIDN'T YOU TELL ME ABOUT THIS SOONER? I WOULD HAVE LOVED YOU TO PRESENT THIS AT THE COMPULSIVE BEHAVIOR CONFERENCE LAST JUNE! Bonnie knew she had a lot to offer; she just didn't seem to want to let anyone else in on the secret. Together we worked on these strategies.

Toot Your Horn With Tact

1. Bring up your achievement in terms of a benefit to your boss, your company, or your colleagues.

"This program I've been working on might be helpful to the accounts receivable department."

199

"This report I worked on might help Nancy get some of the first-quarter figures together."

2. Ask your boss to give an opinion about something that gives evidence of your achievement. Chances are she'll notice what you're proud of.

"Olga, could you check out this layout and let me know if the dimensions seem right?"

3. Put your accomplishment in writing in the form of an update or progress report.

To: Jake W.
From: Bonnie G.
Re: Tape

Just wanted to let you know I've put together a tape on breaking habits, which worked well with fifteen clients. It's available, of course, for staff use.

Consider the old Jewish saying, attributed to Rabbi Hillel:

"If I am not for myself, who will be for me? If I am only for myself, what am I? And if not now, when?"

··········

Awkward
Moments

• I've Forgotten the Name of Someone Who Obviously Knows Me

The *N-A-M-E* technique (see "I Never Remember People's Names After I'm Introduced" on page 39) is designed to prevent this embarrassing predicament. But while you're rooting around without success in your memory banks, it's time for rescue tactics, not self-criticism. Admitting that you can't remember is only one of many options. Most people prefer to avoid looking dumb. So imagine that you are a spy under cover and coolly consider using these Intelligent Name-Recovery Methods.

1. *Ask for Ms. or Mr. Blank's card.* In a business context or with a person who would be very likely to have a business card, this trick may be the easiest to pull off. Make small talk and look for the first opportunity to say something like, "You know, I thought about contacting you the other day and couldn't find your phone number. Could I have your card?"

2. *Ask how to spell the person's name.* Take out a piece of paper and scribble a note to yourself, then look up and ask, "How do you spell your name?" Be ready with humor if he says something like "J-o-h-n."

3. *Create an excuse to have the person write down his or her name and address for you:* "My dog totally destroyed my address book last month, and I'm trying to reconstruct it. Would you write your name and address here for my new one?"

4. *Have the person introduce himself to someone else.* You can orchestrate this situation when someone whose name you do know comes over and wants to be introduced to Ms. Whatever-her-name-is: "Wanda, how nice to see you! This is Wanda Cohen, our second in command, and—" (Point one or both hands, palms up, toward Ms. Whatever-her-name-is and smile. More often than not she'll quickly introduce herself.)

5. *Guess wrong.* If you're on the beach or someplace else

without pencils or business cards, this might be the strategy of choice. It is also helpful when you have forgotten not only the name but also where and in what decade you ever knew this person:

"Ed from Westinghouse, right?"

"No, Don from Digital."

"Of course, of course!"

6. *Admit you've forgotten the name*—but always in a self-deprecating or joking way to avoid offending someone you may have spent hours and hours with not so long ago: "It's really terrible, but I even forget my own name sometimes. It's—"

7. *Ask someone else.* If you think there is an excellent chance that someone else you know knows the name of the lady in black, avoid the issue of names altogether and nudge your buddy afterward and say, "The lady in black—for the life of me I can't remember her name."

• I Dropped Spaghetti on My Shirt While at Lunch With Clients

Remember that others will judge how you handle a disconcerting situation. Dr. Lin, a medical intern, was flying to a residency interview at a hospital when a flight attendant spilled coffee all over her white silk blouse. She hadn't brought along a change of clothes and the stain was very noticeable, but to cancel the hard-earned interview was unthinkable. When her interviewers asked her how the flight was, she told them it was comfortable but there was some sudden turbulence when she was being served coffee. Afterward, the administrator who hired Dr. Lin said, "When I first saw that coffee stain, I felt sorry for you, but when I saw how well you handled the problem, I was impressed. It added to your credentials as far as we were concerned because sometimes it's one emergency after another here."

Recovery Dos and Don'ts for Messy Situations

1. When disaster strikes in a business context, don't allow your discomfort or dry cleaning problem to derail you. Replace the original agenda by sending yourself an internal message like, "This is unfortunate, but I need to go on." Dr. Lin proved a true pro at positive self-talk.

2. Don't make things worse by screaming, complaining, or putting yourself or the perpetrator down. You will look most competent if you excuse yourself and quickly repair the problem as best you can out of sight. One client, a paper manufacturer's representative, lost her temper after a waiter spilled butter sauce on her silk blouse. She is sure she lost a sale because her prospect saw her get so upset.

3. If the disaster happened before your business meeting, call the evidence to your client's or interviewer's attention before she has a chance to notice and judge you for it. One of my attorney clients who walked to work in sneakers and one day forgot her dress shoes made a point of saying to a visitor, "As you can see, I forgot my shoes today."

4. When someone calls to your attention some mustard on your mustache or sauce on your shirt, fix it quickly with a simple "Thanks for letting me know" or a joke, and go on to the next business item.

• How Do I Get My Foot Out of My Mouth?

Communication moments that make us cringe usually don't bring on lasting consequences. That is, not unless you push your foot further into your throat. Milton, a successful photographer, told me he once blew it with a corporate client for whom he had photographed a brochure. In an effort to be personable, he told a company executive that he'd heard his brother was a champion marathon runner. "Not *my* brother," the exec corrected him. "He lost his legs in Vietnam." Milton was so mortified by his faux pas that he cut the conversation short and decided not to continue pursuing this client. Actually, Milton had magnified both the realities and the consequences of his "crime," creating a pretty stiff punishment for himself. There is a better way to cope with an innocent mistake!

To Get Your Foot Out of Your Mouth

1. *Go easy on yourself.* In the worst scenario, the injured party will think your remark is inappropriate or tasteless and perhaps you'll drop a few notches in his estimation for a while. Most likely, though, your conversational partner will sense that what you intended and what you said were not a match, and the incident will pass.

2. *Do internal talking.* The moment after you say something stupid, accept responsibility without putting yourself down too much. Some appropriate self-talk thoughts:

> That was a wrong thing to say.
> It was a mistake but not a disaster.
> I'm feeling embarrassed now. As an adult I can put this in perspective.

3. *Apologize but not too much.* If your conversational partner reacts, corrects, or spits in your face, apologize simply. Examples:

> "Bill, I'm sorry. My comment was insensitive."
>
> "Thanks for correcting me. I ought to have my facts straight before giving a definite opinion."
>
> "Joan, I didn't mean to criticize your boyfriend. Overall, I think he's dynamite."

If you use more than three sentences, however, you're not apologizing but begging for forgiveness. This unfairly puts the injured party in the position of having to comfort *you*.

• She Told Me to Call, but Now She Doesn't Remember Who I Am

Keep in mind that the person you're calling is not sitting around waiting to hear your voice. Instead, you've caught her in the middle of writing a report, fresh off the phone with someone else, balancing her accounts, or daydreaming about her upcoming vacation in Hawaii. Don't take it personally if your name does not inspire immediate recognition. Simply help her remember who you are, where she met you, and why she originally said you should call.

One client, a district manager for a sneakers firm, felt her very personable approach succeeded everywhere but on the telephone. When I listened to her make a call to a prospect, I discovered why. She began the call by saying, "Happy New Year! It's Anita." Anita exaggerated her own importance by expecting her prospect to recognize her by the sound of her voice and a first name. When I showed her how to revamp her phone routine to identify herself more fully, Anita experienced far fewer embarrassing or distressing rejections when she used the phone.

To Help Her Place You

1. After you say who you are, say exactly where and how you first met.

> "This is Len Lerner. We met at the networking party for the Small Business Association in October."

If you really want the caller to feel comfortable, try sending a brief note first, saying you'll be calling.

2. Provide even more fuel for recognition by tying in your meeting with the purpose of the call.

"You mentioned that your company was looking for a guest speaker in the area of time management and suggested I get in touch to share some possible ideas."

3. At times you'll get a cool reception no matter what you say. The fact is that sometimes people tell you to call even though they have no genuine desire to speak with you again. Others may be moody, or you may have caught them at a bad time. As long as they don't hang up on you, follow through on the purpose of your call so they'll remember you the next time.

• I Don't Like to Lie, and I'm Asked About Something I Heard in Confidence

When you are committed to truth telling and a question demands information that you've promised not to give, you need the sly dexterity of a verbal magician. Use the following Houdini tactic to make the noose around your neck disappear.

Slipping Loose When a Question Puts You on the Spot

The situation: Jason Binkley took you out for a drink and confided that he's planning to accept the offer of the presidency of F.G.H. University. "Don't tell anyone I told you—swear? Our negotiations aren't final yet." You swear. The next day your colleague Judy asks, "Do you know what Binkley's planning to do about the F.G.H. offer?"

Answers you don't want to give:

- "No, I don't." That would be a lie and you'd find it hard to say convincingly.
- "Yes, but I can't tell you." That would break your promise and goad Judy to insist that you tell her.
- "Maybe I do, maybe I don't." Very annoying to the questioner.
- "I don't remember." Not believable.
- "I can't answer that question." Tantamount to "yes."

So here's what you do: Change the subject enthusiastically. Evade the question by offering a comment that invites a response or shifts the conversation on to a different track. The enthusiasm distracts or disconcerts your questioner so that even thinking back on the exchange, she's not sure whether you intentionally circumvented the question.

"What a great opportunity for Binkley, huh?"

"I'd take it if I were he, wouldn't you?"

"There was a story about the F.G.H. football coach in the paper the other day—third coach in two years. How can a school have so little pride to put up with such a disaster of an athletic program?"

You can even try a complete switch:

"Listen, I'm worried about Terry, the blonde who works in the mail department. Did you know she carries around enough tranquilizers to kill herself, and she's extremely depressed?"

Unless you're on the witness stand, the maneuver usually works. Practice before you really need it, and you'll find that it's not as difficult to pull off as you might expect. If your questioner seems to catch on to what you're doing or repeats her question, just insist on your new topic. She will think that Binkley bores you or that you're in some mood, and you're off the hook with your integrity intact.

• How Do I Handle Prying Questions, Such as "How's Your Sex Life?"

You don't have to answer a question just because someone asks it! Your first obligation is always to your own sense of dignity and comfort. Whenever a question catches you off guard, makes you uncomfortable, or touches on subjects you don't normally like to talk about, take a moment to assess whether you ought to answer or dodge the question.

Gloria, a friendly small-town woman whose husband had just been elected to a statewide office, learned this lesson the hard way after she agreed to an interview with a young reporter at her home. As a gracious hostess she served the reporter tea and cakes and did her best to make the reporter feel comfortable. Soon she herself felt so comfortable that when the reporter asked whether she had ever regretted being married to a politician, Gloria confided some feelings that she had never discussed with her husband or her close friends. After she recovered from her mortification at seeing those sentiments in print, Gloria came to see me to learn better ways to handle questions that she didn't want to or shouldn't answer.

Strategies for No-Revelations, No-Regrets Responses to Prying Questions

1. *Polite refusal:* "I know a lot of people don't mind talking about their lingerie, but I guess I'm a little old-fashioned."
2. *Humor:* "I can't tell you *all* my secrets."
3. *Exaggeration:* "We have sex three times before every meal—doesn't everyone?"
4. *Close relative excuse:* "Even my wife doesn't know whether the book is autobiographical."

"Even my hairdresser doesn't know for sure what my natural hair color is."

5. *Confession of embarrassment:* "I have to be honest—I feel rather embarrassed by your question."

6. *Throwing the question back:* "I'm not going to tell you how I'm voting, but anyone who knows me well could guess."

7. *Questioning the question:* "I really have to wonder why anyone would ask me whether or not I used drugs in college."

8. *Putting up a barrier:* "I plead the fifth."

"Morley, you know I can't discuss my relationship with the chairman. There's a court case pending."

9. *Vagueness:* "How much do I make? Enough."

"I wouldn't call myself rich, but I get by."

"I'd say somewhere in the five-figure range."

....

We're Not
Communicating

• People Always Interrupt Me

In everyday conversation it's normal to have a degree of interruption going both ways. It's especially common for people to
begin a comment just as another speaker is finishing his. Conversational researchers refer to this as "overlap." But if you're
never doing the interrupting and are always receiving it, something is wrong. Let's consider first some different causes of
Conversation Interruptus.

One possibility is that you misperceive normal overlap as an
interruption and don't realize you can just keep talking. In
effect, you are yielding the floor much too easily or too often.

Another possibility is that your style of conversation makes
people want to talk more than listen. Are you being boring,
long-winded, tentative; are you digressing too much? Are you
failing to signal clearly when you're finished and when you're
not? Is the pause between your thoughts too long? These are all
reasons why people might feel the urge to interrupt you. You
might also be making them so enthusiastic that they can't hold
in their reaction.

Interruptions have a lot to do, too, with power dynamics
and sex differences in communication. Many studies have
shown that the person with higher status in a relationship (such
as a teacher with a pupil) interrupts more. Researchers have
found that in male-female conversations, males do most of the
interrupting. Not only that, women tend to embellish topics
men bring up, while men frequently just ignore topics raised by
women.

Remedies for Victims of Conversation
Interruptus

1. Observe the pattern of interruptions. Then experiment
with talking through what you perceive as an interruption,

without raising your voice. The who-yields-to-whom ratio should grow more equal. Everybody in everyday conversation gets interrupted—don't take it personally!

2. Control your body language and style and pace of conversation. Close your mouth when you're finished; drop your pitch at the end of your last sentence. Explicitly throw the conversation back to the other person with a question ("Do you agree?"). This will give you more control of the conversation. Don't let more than five seconds of silence go by in the middle of your turn, or people will assume you have nothing more to say.

3. With someone more powerful, yield. Wait for a natural break in the conversation and then jump right in. In 1988, during a confrontational live interview between CBS anchorman Dan Rather and then vice president and presidential candidate George Bush, both men kept on talking. Most observers blamed Rather, not Bush, for failing to yield.

4. If a person who has equal status with you keeps on interrupting out of aggressiveness, insensitivity, or dominance, stand your ground. Raise your index finger to signal "Wait" and keep on talking. If that doesn't work, wag your finger and say, "I'd like to finish." Or approach the person before the conflict has a chance to heat up and say, "When we talk, I notice you interrupt me much more than I interrupt you. I'd like you to let me finish more."

• I Ramble a Lot

Then it's time to get on course because you're undoubtedly driving people crazy! To get to your destination without wandering, first figure out what's happening when you stray. Ramblers often provide too much detail, add comments that are tangential to the topic at hand, or have difficulty knowing when their talking turn is finished.

Anne, a fiction writer and poet, came to see me about her conversational style. I found her stream-of-consciousness style of speaking hard to follow. Within our first half hour she had discussed her poetry, pets, mother-in-law, landlord problems, and their relation to the universe. When I intervened by requesting, "Could you say your main reason for coming here in fifteen words or less?" she said, "Because I don't know what the heck I'm trying to say half the time." Aha! She was delighted to learn methods to cut her own and her conversational partners' confusion.

Rules to Help Ramblers Go Straight

1. Don't let comments exceed forty-five seconds or one minute.

2. Rein yourself in so that you stay with one topic at a time.

3. Whenever you bring up a new topic, introduce it with a transition phrase so that your listener will know where you're coming from.

> "In addition to my problems with whether or not to keep my cats, I've also had trouble lately with my landlord."

4. Trim the fat by mentally discriminating between what your listener would and wouldn't want to hear about a given topic. Example: mental checklist about landlords.

Laurie would be interested in: the fight I had with the landlord; other living arrangement options.

Laurie could not care less about: the twelve things wrong with my sink; what my brother in Chicago said.

Sharpen your discrimination skills by taping a conversation and playing it back to judge the relevancy and interest value of your comments. Take the perspective of your listener and be a tough critic.

5. If you bring up a topic and perceive signs that your listener is not tuned in, it's better to drop it than drone on. (For these signs, see "I'm Never Sure Whether Someone Wants to Keep Talking to Me" on page 51.)

6. Start thinking mind over mouth. Construct a mental map of your main point or conclusion and how you plan to get there. The "Instant Recipes" in "What If I Have Only a Minute to Prepare Some Remarks?" (page 155) should help.

7. Ask close colleagues or friends to signal if you need to get to the point or if you've held the floor too long. When in doubt, stop!

• I Always Get Blank Looks When I Speak

If you're concerned about audiences' expressionless stares, see "I Get Freaked Out When an Audience Stares Blankly at Me" (page 101). If you receive more than an occasional blank look when you're conversing one on one, you're probably doing something that prevents your message from getting through. Let's explore the possibilities.

Your vocabulary or sentence structure may need adjustment if it's too technical, abstract, or pompous. For example, many lawyers speak "legalese," a version of English filled with henceforths, parties of the seventh part, and clauses tacked on to each other ad infinitum. Since many listeners won't let you know when you're speaking above their heads, it's up to you to translate for them. Check in with listeners occasionally to make sure you're communicating. Questions such as "Am I being clear?" and "Is there anything you'd like me to explain?" let you take responsibility for remedying communication breakdowns.

Another reason for glazed gazes might be that you have little facial animation yourself, and listeners are simply mirroring you. Research indicates that a speaker who uses various facial expressions is perceived as more engaging and influential. Mentally observe yourself during conversations to see if you're giving what you receive.

It's also possible that your listeners are masking with a frozen face their embarrassment about a mannerism you use while speaking. Over the years my clients who stutter have told me that when people don't know how to react, they just stare. Other communication behaviors that produce listener discomfort include too many pauses, peculiar facial expressions or sounds (one client clicked his tongue whenever he was thinking), and frequent mispronunciations. Gather the courage to ask someone who knows you well if there is anything disconcerting about the way you speak.

Mumbling, speaking too fast, speaking softly, or speaking with a strong accent can sometimes reduce intelligibility to the point where no one can catch what you're saying. To rule out these factors, consult the sections on "People Often Ask Me to Repeat Myself" (page 8), "I Talk Too Fast" (page 11), "People Can't Hear Me" (page 15), and "Aside From Changing My Foreign Accent, Can I Help People Understand Me Better?" (page 233).

There remains the small possibility that your thoughts are so interesting that listeners become lost in them. I'll never forget the gentleman who sat in the front row at a talk I gave at the American Speech-Language-Hearing Association Convention in Detroit several years ago. He stared strangely at me throughout my forty-five-minute talk and left the moment I finished. I was sure he was angry or troubled by my presentation. Two weeks later, however, the very same fellow called me to say that my presentation was the most "refreshing" one at the convention. Stunned and gratified, I told him I'd assumed from his negative facial expression that he'd hated it. "Oh, that," he said. "My grimaces. That's how I always look when I'm really thinking."

• What Do I Do When We're Just Not Clicking?

Even the best communicators don't hit it off with everyone they meet. Yet good communicators are *always* aware of rough spots in an interaction that require fixing or adjustment. To prevent frustration and bafflement from escalating to unfair judgments and inappropriate decisions, use the following manual.

Diagnostic Tips and Communication Repair Procedures

1. When you're not clicking with someone, consider whether there's a difference in communication style. This list of some common contrasts may help.

- X talks a mile a minute and uses rapid gestures; Y talks slowly, moves slowly.
- X is blunt; Y prefers to be subtle.
- X offers many signals of interest; Y maintains a poker face.
- X is no-nonsense, to the point; Y is anecdotal, expansive.
- X jokes a lot; Y is a serious guy.
- X has a polished, professional image; Y is sloppy, casual.
- X is demonstrative and emotional; Y is rational, cool.

2. Monitor yourself. Observe the interaction as if you were behind a one-way mirror, asking yourself, What's wrong with this picture? Examples:

Hmm, I'm asking all the questions, and he's giving monosyllabic answers.

She's wearing a sad expression while I'm babbling on about my fabulous weekend.

I'm cracking jokes, and he's not laughing.

3. Identify a change that you can make. This won't make you phony, only flexible.

I'll lean back and refrain from asking additional questions.

I'll slow down and give her a chance to share what's on her mind if she wants to.

I'll get serious for a change and see how he responds.

4. Make a "break the ice" statement if you think it will help. Remember, you take responsibility for improving communication without blaming your conversational partner.

"I know I've been firing a lot of questions at you. Why don't we just stop here so you can bring up your concerns?"

"Jennie, is something bothering you?"

> **Good communication is not a matter of chance; It's a matter of choice**

• People Say I Look Angry (Sad, Bored), but I'm Not

The angry, sad, or bored face someone shows to the world is what he's judged by, regardless of how he feels inside. Mirrors, photographs, videotapes, and the reactions you usually get from others provide hints about whether or not you often project moods that contradict your feelings.

Joanne came to see me because she was fed up with her nonimpact on people. Though she was well dressed and well groomed, even her psychiatrist found her boring. It wasn't hard to see why. No matter what she was saying, her eyes would be half closed, her face deadpan and expressionless. Joanne was anxious to improve her social and professional life, so she was glad to learn that there *was* a quick fix for her problem.

The Quick-Fix Face for First Impressions

Follow these two steps in front of a mirror.

1. *Lip curl.* Curl up the corners of your lips in a half smile. Your goal is a pleasant, not ecstatic, expression.

2. *Eye-opener.* Widen your eyes just a little to add alertness and sparkle, but don't stare or change your blinking pattern. Your goal is to look interested in your environment and others.

Now you're ready to face people.

After several weeks of Quick-Fix Face practice, Joanne "modeled" her new expression for her therapist, who said it was a dramatic lift from her usual sad-sack face. She also reported that at a progressive dinner one man said she was fun to talk to. Unbelievable, she told me; before, everyone had always wanted to "progress" beyond her.

• People Say I Seem Standoffish, but I'm Really Shy

Although snobbishness and shyness are attitudinal opposites, they stem from the same root cause—uncomfortableness and insecurity. Shy people express their insecurity by thinking, No one could possibly want to deal with me. Snobs, on the other hand, express theirs by thinking, I don't want to deal with anyone unless he's the right kind of person. These two very different attitudes often look the same at first glance because both the snooty and the shy tend to look away from people and wear an unpleasant expression.

I once worked with Amy, a gifted teacher who loved children and was eager to form positive relationships with her students' parents. She was devastated to learn that several parents had described her to the principal as aloof and cold. The minute I met Amy, I could see why. She held her head sideways, peered at me suspiciously, and shook my hand without a smile. As I got to know and like Amy, she told me that she felt shy about giving advice to parents. She had no idea that her stance seemed standoffish. Apparently she had attended a boarding school where girls learned these postures as good etiquette.

With the help of a full-length mirror and videotaping, Amy began to adjust her style. It really took only minute changes in her facial expression and position. Warming up is a great way to describe what shy people need to do (and snobby people as well, if they care to).

To warm up:

1. Make good face contact. If you are afraid to look people in the eye, that's all right—look at their noses instead, and you'll get as good a reception.

2. Practice wearing a pleasant facial expression, as de-

scribed in "People Say I Look Angry (Sad, Bored), but I'm Not" (page 225). Twitching a few facial muscles differently usually does wonders.

3. Act like a confident, warm person and it's likely that that's how you will be perceived.

• I Get Embarrassed When I'm Complimented

When someone goes out of her way to offer a sincere comment designed to let you know you're special, swell, or savvy, don't make her feel as if she's said something gauche or unacceptable. You can train yourself to accept the compliment rather than toss it off. This way you allow the complimenter to glow in her own good will. And you? Well, you just might learn to value what others value in you.

When a Gush Makes You Blush

1. *Inhibit your impulse to deny, debate, or diffuse the compliment.* Prohibited phrases:

> "Thanks, but it was nothing."
> "You really like it? How could you?"
> "I just bought it for a nickel at a yard sale."
> "It's no big deal."
> "Are you kidding?"

Instead, talk to yourself before responding. Notice and comment on how you feel.

> It's a compliment, and I feel embarrassed.
> Hold on, you can take it. It's only a compliment.
> I need to make her feel good about complimenting me.

2. *Beginner's-level compliment taking.*

> "Thanks, I appreciate that."
> "That's a nice thought—thanks."
> "I'm glad you like it."
> Or simply, "Thanks!"

3. *Advanced compliment taking* (when you feel comfortable with the beginner's level and truly appreciate the compliment). *Add a comment of your own:*

"Thanks for noticing. It was hard work to lose twenty pounds."

Explore the compliment. Try to find out more about the traits your complimenter appreciates, a particularly useful technique when the compliment concerns your work:

"Thanks for your kind note about the Jones proposal. Which parts did you feel were most persuasive?"

And don't forget to compliment yourself for gracefully accepting the compliment!

• I Try to Motivate My Employees, but They Seem to Be Intimidated

Probably your method of directing staff comes across as author-itarian or manipulative. Human beings naturally resist efforts to control their behavior (have you ever tried to persuade a four-year-old to eat broccoli?). If you have a "Because I say so" attitude, your staff may comply, but you won't get the quality work that you would with a more positive style. If you want to motivate rather than intimidate your staff, refrain from using the following:

- Loud or sarcastic tone of voice
- Blaming sentences:

  "Why didn't you—"
  "How could you—"
  "I'm surprised you didn't—"

- Comparison to others:

  "Toby Waldman always left the files in decent order."
  "Most people I know with Ivy League degrees can do this kind of a math problem."

- Strong negative emotions:

  "I'm sick of everyone taking advantage of me."
  "Your smoking is ruining our image and giving me cancer."

If you as the boss can project a "We're all in this together" attitude, you'll elicit productivity and enthusiasm. Try these methods to tone down your Big Bad Boss image and get the team moving:

1. *Hedging.* Purposely act and sound unsure about the re-quest you're making.

"I know you have a lot to do, but maybe you'll be able to get to the Downs account by three?"

(People respond better to requests than to commands.)

2. *Valued opinion.* Solicit your employee's opinion and let her do it her way whenever possible. (After all, your main goal is to get it done.)

"Fredrika, we need to lay out the Christmas catalog by Wednesday. What suggestions do you have for graphics?"

3. *Softening.* Mr. Rogers, not Attila the Hun, should be your role model here. Purposely turn down the volume, hesitate a bit, tilt your head just a tinge, and you'll be easier to take.

Caution: Use these methods consciously and with care. Never change your style without knowing what your aim is.

• I Have Trouble Understanding Foreign Accents

Few communication situations are as frustrating as straining to understand exotic pronunciation patterns. Despite concentration and good will, you can fail to catch even islands of sense in a stream of mysterious sounds. But there are alternatives to tuning out, and over time, many people manage to adapt to once unfamiliar accents.

To Decipher English With a Foreign Ring

1. Watch the speaker for nonverbal clues to meaning. One study attributed only 7 percent of what is communicated orally to the words and the rest to tone of voice, gestures, and facial expressions.

2. Chances are that a hard-to-understand speaker will want to know that she's not getting through. I've worked with foreign-born professors who were devastated to learn only at the end of the term that many students had had problems comprehending them. In conversation, ask for clarification:

> "I'm having a little trouble understanding you. Would you mind repeating that a little more slowly?"
>
> "I got you up to the part about the tattoo. Would you mind going over the rest of the story again?"
>
> "Did you mean we need to get *close,* as in nearer?"

In a context such as a university course, students can ask the hard-to-understand professor to provide detailed handouts of class notes. Any sort of supplementary visual aids would help them follow along.

3. Unless certain details are critical for you to understand, if you have gotten the essence of the message, let the rest of it go.

• Aside From Changing My Foreign Accent, Can I Help People Understand Me Better?

As you no doubt have discovered, people differ in their ability to understand an unfamiliar accent. You're likely to have smoother conversations with Americans who have met others from your background, are interested in different cultures, or have learned other languages themselves. Unfortunately, most Americans now fall woefully short when it comes to foreign languages. It is your responsibility to determine how well you're getting your message across and to be willing to adjust your speaking style to enhance communication.

How to Help the Natives Understand You Better

1. *Rate reduction.* Though you may not really be talking too fast, slowing down can help limited listeners absorb the message. Say "one-two" to yourself at the end of phrases, word groups, and sentences. Go especially slowly on names of people, places, and companies.

2. *Volume control.* Though I know people sometimes shout at you, foolishly thinking it will help you understand English better, maintaining a loud enough volume consistently on *your* part will at least eliminate any complaint that they can't *hear* you. Ask an American (with normal hearing) to give feedback on your volume as you engage in conversation in a moderately noisy environment. Have your friend signal to you to increase volume until your message comes across completely.

3. *Be alert to confusion signals.* When your listener looks puzzled or blank, or responds with something totally unrelated

to what you just said, it's a good bet that she didn't get it. Same thing if she nods in approval when you announce you're thinking of jumping off the Golden Gate Bridge. Some folks feel funny admitting they haven't the foggiest notion of what you just said.

4. *Repeat and rephrase.* Give important information more than once, so your listener has more than one chance to interpret what you've said.

> "It happened when I was driving on Mass Ave., not very fast, and a van came out of the side street without stopping at the stop sign. The van pulled out of the small street onto Mass Ave. in front of my car . . ."

5. *Say more rather than less.* The more context you include, the easier it is for listeners to understand a strange-sounding word. Kent, a New Englander, stopped in a small town in Arkansas while on a cross-country trip and had the following exchange with a store owner:

"Do you have oil?"

"Do we have what?"

"Oil. Oil [pronounced *oyl*]."

Blank look from the store owner.

"Oil. You know, motor oil for my car?"

"Oh, *erl*. Erl. Of course we got erl . . ."

6. *Extend permission to interrupt* you if your listener isn't certain what you've said.

> "People sometimes have a hard time with my accent. Please feel free to ask me to repeat."

7. *Check periodically* to make sure the message has been received.

> "Is there anything you'd like me to review?"
> "Do you get the picture?"

• My Colleague Never Listens to Me

Though you can't make someone a better listener, you can make yourself a person more likely to be listened to. David, a product manager for a well-known brand of cookies, would crumble every time he had to give an update to Bernard, who was in charge of European sales. As David told me at our first meeting, Bernard would look into space while David was speaking and then start in on a completely different point. David decided on a three-part strategy to encourage Bernard to tune in.

1. He opened his remarks with an attention getter to capture Bernard's initial interest. Research indicates that in order to get mute males to engage in conversation, their female partners use grabber phrases such as "Oh, did you hear about . . ." "You won't believe what happened to me," or "Listen to this." Here's how David translated this technique into the business context:

> "There are three critical points I want to let you in on."
> "There's some confidential information about our new double creamies without cholesterol that I want to share with you."

2. David would not speak unless Bernard was making reasonable eye contact. At first this produced some awkward ten-second pauses. Then Bernard learned to look at David if he didn't want to sit in silence. David reported that Bernard seemed to respect him for letting on that he had a right to be listened to.

3. By asking an opinion or review question David would get Bernard to acknowledge the points David had made before moving on.

> "What's your opinion about my suggestion to include a coupon for a free ice cream cone in the cookie box?"

"What do you think are the strong and weak parts of the cookie-box proposal?"

To review, if you have someone in your life who listens like a loon, try David's ideas for dealing with poor listeners.

1. Begin your comment with a grabber.
2. Don't speak until you have the wayward listener's full attention.
3. Ask questions that require effective listening in order to be answered well.

• I'm Not a Good Listener

At least you admit it! When I ask clients what they consider their greatest communication strength, the most frequent response is, "I'm a good listener." Yet few of us are actually very skilled at tuning in.

Kingsley, a young salesman in the fast-paced medical equipment field, came to see me after customers complained to his boss that he monopolized their time and had trouble getting orders straight. During our initial session, Kingsley talked nonstop, even cutting me off when I asked a question—about how poor a listener people said he was. On the way out he commented that I was a super listener. I didn't tell him that like the four walls I was simply a captive audience.

Kingsley was a tough case. He first needed to improve his talk/listen ratio—talking less and listening more. If he never shut up, there was nothing to listen to. I began working with him by setting up some artificial rules for conversation. He would begin to talk to me, and after thirty seconds, no matter where he was in his story, he would have to end his sentence and ask me a question. In this way he experienced what it was like not to be talking all the time. After achieving a more balanced talk/listen ratio, I taught him the *E-A-R* technique to get him started on the road toward effective listening.

The *E-A-R* technique involves three steps that begin to improve poor listening habits:

Empathize. Commit yourself to understanding (not necessarily agreeing with) your conversational partner's point of view. The late psychologist and father of active or deep listening, Carl Rogers, believed that an *attitude* of empathy toward a conversational partner was more important than any behavior. With this attitude you are at least trying to tune in to your partner's wavelength.

Attend. Give full nonverbal attention to your partner:

- Focus your eyes on his face.
- When he pauses, encourage with *uh-huh*s and *mm-hmm*s.
- Show a slight forward lean (about 20 degrees).
- Try not to fidget, glance away, or adjust your posture.

Many people who are said to possess charisma, from Jacqueline Kennedy Onassis to Burt Reynolds, are gifted attenders. In their presence you feel as if you're the most charming person alive—and the other 110 people in the room feel the same way.

Respond. Good listening includes talking that indicates you've heard or understood your partner's message or feelings. Use response phrases like these to show that you've "gotten it":

"That sounds [exciting, challenging, disappointing, and so forth]."

"I know what you mean about [that awful committee, Melinda's crazy schedule]."

"Let me see if I understood everything. You're saying that [business will be on the upswing come April, you're confused about our wedding plans]."

If after using one of these response phrases, your partner comments, "That's right" or "That's exactly what I mean," congratulations! You've left your poor listening habits behind.

Index

Abdominal breathing, 25–26
Accents
   foreign, 232–34
   regional, 30–32
Accomplishments, letting boss know about, 199–200
Agendas for meetings, 162
Age of voice, 33–34
Annoying behavior, 185–86
Answering machines, 80–81
Answering the telephone, 67–68
Anxiety. *See* Nervousness
Apologizing, 35
Argumentative people, 191–92
Articulation, 3
Assimilation, 8–9
Audience participation, 136–37
Audience psychology, 101–2
Authoritative speech, 35–36

Blanking out, 95–96
   notes as insurance against, 112
Blank looks, 221
Boss
   over-monitoring by, 177–78
   tooting your horn to, 199–200
Brainstorming, 137
Breaking dates, 189–90
Breaks
   during meetings, 164
   during presentations, 146
Breathiness, 22
Breathing, 25–26
   One-two technique and, 11
   stress-control, 91
   volume and, 16
Buzz sessions, 136–37

Call-waiting, 72
Charismatic speakers, 148

Charts, 128, 129
Chatterers, 54
Clip-on microphones, 131
Closeness, 107, 108
Comfort in front of group, 91
Coming attractions, 111
Communication repair procedures, 223–24
Compliments, learning to take, 228–29
Condolences, 193–94
Confidence collapse, 93
Confidences, keeping, 211–12
Conspicuousness, 103
Conversations
   beginning, 45–46
   cooled, 51
   ending, 58–59
   keeping going, 56–57
   shifting, 52
   skills, 53–55
Criticism
   accepting, 171
   giving, 172–73

Dates, breaking, 189–90
Decision making, 160–61
Decor for presentation, 146
Demonstrations, 137
Discrimination instruction, 31–32

E-A-R technique, 237
Emotions, appealing to, 111
Enriching your voice, 33–34
Environment for presentation, 145–47
Exaggeration, humorous, use of, 120
Excess talking, 195–96

Eye contact
 with audience, 115–17
 poor, 36

Facial expression, 225
Famous people, approaching, 62–
  63
Fast talkers, 11–12
Fatigue zones, 146
Faux pas, recovering from, 207–8
Feedback, tactful, 178
Feelers, 53–54
Fielding questions, 138–39
Fight-or-flight response, 90
Fillers, 7
Flip charts, 128
Foreign accents, 232–34
Formality, 103
"Fry," 19

Gestures, 118–19
Giggling, 36
Going blank, fear of, 94–96
Greetings, telephone, 67–68
Grief, psychology of, 193–94
Groups
 breaking into, 41–42
 introducing yourself to, 103–4

Hand-held microphone, 131
Hedging, 35
Hold, putting callers on, 71–72
Hostile questions, 140–42
Humor in presentations, 120–21

Idiotic questions, 140–42
Inappropriate behavior, 185–86
Incompetent employees, dealing
  with, 181–82
Interpreters, 197–98
Interruptions, 217–18
Introducing yourself to group,
  103–4
Introductions of speakers, 122–23

Job interviews
 posture during, 175–76
 selling yourself in, 174
Jokes, 120
Jumbling words, 8

"Kiss-and-smile" exercise, 27

Lavaliere microphone, 131
Lecterns, 147
Length change, 6
Lighting, 145–47
Listening, effective, 235–38

Major theme, extracting, 111
Meetings
 breaks during, 164
 decision making during, 160–
  61
 expressing opinions in, 157
 handling difficult people in,
  165–67
 meandering, 162–63
 orchestrating, 153–54
 time wasting at, 158–59
Messy situations, 205–6
Microphones, 130–31
Mind-over-mouth quickie, 27
Mirroring, 176
Motivating employees, 230–31
Mouth
 mobilization of, 9–10
 morning, 27
Movement, excessive, 36

Names
 forgotten, embarrassment over,
  203–4
 techniques for remembering, 39
Nasality, 21
National Stuttering Project, 137
Naturalness, 107, 108
Nervousness, 85–104
 audience perception of, 97–98

audience psychology and, 101–2
controlling, 90–93
counteracting, 88
getting rid of, 85–86
over going blank, 94–96
identifying causes of, 87–88
physical manifestations of, 99–100
practical actions to combat, 89
rational look at, 88
success thoughts and, 89
troubleshooting, 88
Notes
eye contact and, 116–17
speaking from, 94, 112–14

One-minute scan, 115
One-on-one communication, 107–8
One-two technique, 11
Opening exercise, 27
Openness Openers, 49–50
Opinions, expressing, 157
Orchestrating meetings, 153–54
Organization of talk, 109–11
Overassimilation, 8–9

Pacing, 13–14
Pauses, 7
  One-two technique and, 11
Performance anxiety. *See* Nervousness
Personal space, violations of, 183–84
Persuasion, 191–92
Phonetics, 3
Pick-a-tic technique, 86
Pitch
  changing, 5
  high, 36
  lowering, 19–20
  raised at end of statement, 35
Plosives, 3–4
Plus Arrow Plus technique, 59

Plus-Minus-Plus method, 172–73, 178
Practical action, urging audience to take, 111
Precision, 10
Preparing for speech, 94
Presentation
  anxiety about, *see* Nervousness
  audience participation in, 136–37
  eye contact during, 115–17
  fielding questions during, 138–39
  gestures during, 118–19
  humor in, 120–21
  introduction before, 122–23
  microphones for, 130–31
  notes for, 112–14
  one-on-one communication versus, 107–8
  organizing, 109–11
  room arrangements for, 132–35
  stage managing for success of, 145–47
  sticking to prepared material for, 143–44
  style for, 148–49
  visual aids in, 127–29
  warming up an audience for, 124–26
Projection, 34
Prompts, 49
Posture
  during job interview, 176
  poor, 36

Qualifying, 35
Questions
  about confidences, 211–12
  open, 50
  during presentation, 137–42
  prying, 213–14
Quick-Fix Face technique, 225
Quiz for audience members, 136

Rambling, 219–20
Rapid speech, 11–12
Real-life examples, humorous, 120–21
Receptivity signals, 43–44
Regionalism, 30–32
Rehearsing speeches, 94
Relaxation techniques, 90–93
Remarks, instant recipes for, 155–56
Repetition burnout, 187–88
Resonance, 33
Responsiveness, 107, 108
Room arrangements, 132–35
"Rule of Three," 115

Secretaries, dealing with, over telephone, 69–70
Self-deprecation, 121
Selling, 179–80
Sexual harassment, 61
Shyness, overcoming, 226–27
Silent pauses, 7
Slides, 128
Slow speech, 13–14
Small talk, 47–48
Smiling, excessive, 36
Smoking, 146
  stopping, 23
Soft voice, 15–16
Spatial relationships, 183–84
Speed-up strategies, 14
Stage managing presentations, 145–47
Standing, 34
Stand-up microphone, 131
Stationary microphone, 131
Stops, 4
Stress-control breathing, 91
Stretching for success, 92–93

Success shake, 92
Switching tracks, 52

Talkativeness, excessive, 195–96
Tape, hearing yourself on, 28–29
T-E-A-M approach to selling, 179–80
Telephone
  answering, at work, 67–68
  answering machines, 80–81
  calling strangers, 76–77
  coworkers and, 73
  forgetting subject of call, 78
  getting past secretary, 69–70
  getting someone's attention over, 74–75
  identifying oneself on, 209–10
  putting caller on hold, 71–72
  tag, 79
Thin vocal quality, 36
Touching, 60–61
Trailing-off sentences, 8
Translations, 197–98

"Um" and "uh" extermination, 7
Uncomfortable situations, recovering from, 205–6

Visual aids, 127–29
Vocal health, maintaining, 23
Vocal variety, 5–6
Voice trouble, signs of, 23
Volume
  changes in, 5–6
  controlling, 17–18
  dropping, 8
  increasing, 15–16
Vowels, 10

Warming up before presentation, 115
"Wave, the," 92